Birgit Bellis

Advanced Student Guide

Education, Prevention & Mitigation for Violence in the Workplace

David Fowler

Founder and Author of
Workplace Violence Training Programs

Incidence + Response = outcome

AVADE® Advanced Student Guide

Education, Prevention & Mitigation for Violence in the Workplace

Disclaimer

The author and the publisher, Personal Safety Training, Inc., do not dictate policies or procedures for the use of any violence prevention, self-defense or any physical intervention authorized for use by a department/agency or private individual. The suggestions/options disseminated in this book are simply that, suggestions or options. Each individual, department or agency is responsible for developing their own "policies and procedures" regarding the use of violence prevention, self-defense and physical intervention for their personnel and for themselves. Although every effort has been made for this book to be complete and accurate, it is impossible to predict, discuss or plan for every circumstance or situation which might arise in the course of defending yourself and any contact with a violent or aggressive person(s) or during a crime.

Every reader must always take into consideration their experience, physical abilities, professional responsibilities, agency and department procedures and state, local and federal legal requirements. With this in mind, each reader must evaluate the recommendations and techniques contained in this book and decide for himself (herself) which should be used and under what circumstances. Each reader assumes risk of loss, injury, and damages associated with this book and use of the information obtained in it. The author and publisher, Personal Safety Training, Inc., cannot guarantee or warrant the legal, medical, tactical or technical suggestions/options in this book. **ANY IMPLIED WARRANTIES ARE EXPRESSLY DISAVOWED.**

Personal Safety Training Inc.
Telephone: (208) 691-7481
www.AVADEtraining.com
www.PersonalSafetyTraining.com

Also by David Fowler

Violence In The Workplace, Be Safe Not Sorry, To Serve and Protect

Acknowledgement

I would like to thank the many teachers, instructors, mentors and friends that have helped make this program a reality. Without your help, inspiration and invaluable knowledge this wouldn't have been possible. To all of you, I am eternally grateful.

I would also like to thank the thousands of individuals that I have worked with whose direct and indirect contribution to this program has made it possible for me to do what I feel on purpose to do.

Special thanks to the following individuals for their support and technical advice: Jason Blessinger, Jean Boles, Mark Costello, Genelle Fowler, Brian Goodwin, Brian Keltz, Mark Loudin, Steve Petillo, Eduardo Montez and Mark Mooring.

I would also like to thank my family for their support; I love you all so much!

David

David Fowler
Founder, AVADE® Personal Safety Training & Workplace Violence Prevention Programs
President, Personal Safety Training Inc.

CONTENTS

Introduction

Incidents of Workplace Violence happen every second, minute and hour of each day in the United States. OSHA and the CDC have declared that workplace violence is now an epidemic in some industries. Hospitals, government, law enforcement and corporate security continue to tighten down, but there are steps YOU can take, as an individual, to protect yourself from violence while on the job.

Education, Prevention and Mitigation

The **AVADE® WPV Prevention Training** is designed to educate, prevent and mitigate the risk of violence to individuals in the workplace.

The AVADE® WPV Prevention training program meets the requirements of State and Federal guidelines, as well as OSHA's General Duty Clause, to provide employees with a workplace free from recognized hazards likely to cause death or serious physical harm.
*AVADE® training also meets the Joint Commission's regulatory compliance for maintaining a workplace violence prevention training program.

An employer's overall plan should include administrative, behavioral and environmental strategies to prevent and mitigate the risk of workplace violence. The AVADE® training course provides this level of education and will also empower you to:

- Identify workplace violence risk factors
- Recognize emerging situations before they turn violent
- Deal with an agitated or dangerous individual
- De-escalate individuals who are: stressed, intoxicated, angry or combative
- Escape and survive a workplace violence incident
- Respond appropriately to an emergent situation
- Survive an active shooter situation
- And more…

The **AVADE® Workplace Violence Prevention Training Program** was researched and developed to be the most complete and effective workplace violence prevention training program for the corporate and healthcare environment. The **AVADE® WPV Prevention Training Program** is tailored specifically to the unique needs and dynamics of the workplace.

Have YOU been a victim of Workplace Violence?

Have you ever…
- Been Verbally Harassed?
- Intimidated by Someone?
- Threatened by Someone?
- Received Obscene Phone Calls?
- Had Property Damage?
- Been Robbed (Robbery)?
- Received a Bomb Threat?
- Had Someone Verbally Assault You?
- Witnessed a completed or attempted Suicide?
- Been Stalked by Someone?
- Had a Road Rage Situation?
- Experienced Gang Violence?
- Been Physically Assaulted?
    - Pushed, Shoved, Grabbed, Kicked or Slapped
    - Edged Weapon or Guns
    - Sexual Assault
- Take Hostage/Kidnapped?
- Threatened with a Weapon?
- Been involved in a Terrorism Incident?

If you answered YES to any of the above questions, you have witnessed or experienced workplace violence.

Workplace Violence Defined
Workplace violence is any act of aggression, verbal assault, physical assault, or threatening behavior that occurs in the workplace environment and causes physical or emotional harm to guests, staff or visitors.

The National Institute for Occupational Safety and Health Administration (NIOSH) and the Occupational Safety and Health Administration (OSHA) define workplace violence as any physical assault, threatening behavior or verbal abuse occurring in the workplace. Violence includes overt and covert behaviors ranging in aggressiveness from verbal harassment to murder. (NIOSH, OSHA).

There are several dangerous myths about workplace violence. Knowing the truth will help you to be better prepared if you ever face an incident of workplace violence.

The Myths of Workplace Violence

1. It won't happen here!
2. There is nothing we can do about it.
3. Management and the Agency just don't care.

Myth #1: That would never happen where I work.
In the early 1990s, the phrase "going postal" entered the American lexicon, after eleven post office shootings left thirty-five people dead between 1983 and 1993. Contrary to that slang term, however, workplace violence is not confined to post offices, or any one industry. Workplace violence can happen at any place of employment, with social services and healthcare being the highest in non-fatal assaults against employees.

Learning the **AVADE®** principles will help keep you, and others stay safe.

Myth #2: There's nothing you can do about it. People just snap. You can't predict it.
This is, perhaps, the most dangerous myth about workplace violence. Do a little research on almost ANY incident of workplace violence and you will quickly see that the perpetrator gave warning signals. In virtually every case, there were signs that the violent person was escalating and about to perpetrate a crime. The only caveat to this is, we don't always have the opportunity to see the signs. A person may just walk into your place of business and go off. Healthcare, law enforcement and the security industries are more prevalent to this as their work is based on emergent needs.

Prevention is the key to creating a safe and friendly environment for guests and visitors, as well as a safer workplace for staff. It is possible to prevent and reduce the effects of violence. The most important step is to establish a comprehensive program in the workplace, dedicated to educating, preventing, mitigating, tracking incidents, and providing support for those affected.

Myth #3: My employer doesn't care.
Employers do understand the risks and do care. Many employers are adopting policies and procedures for preventing workplace violence. Aside from the human cost, workplace violence costs businesses a lot of money.

The Cost of Workplace Violence

- The cost to US business from workplace violence is estimated at more than $120 billion a year.

- Costs of non-fatal workplace assaults: 876,000 lost workdays per year, $16 million in lost wages per year.

- The average jury award, in subsequent liability cases where the employer failed to take proactive, preventive measures under OSHA guidelines, is $3.1 million per person, per incident.

OSHA

Currently, there is no federal standard that requires workplace violence protections. However, The **Occupational Safety and Health Act of 1970** (OSH Act)1 mandates that, in addition to compliance with hazard-specific standards, all employers have a general duty to provide their employees with a workplace free from recognized hazards likely to cause death or serious physical harm.

OSHA will rely on Section 5a-1 of the OSH Act, the "**General Duty Clause**," for enforcement authority. Failure to implement these guidelines is not in itself a violation of the General Duty Clause; however, employers can be cited for violating the General Duty Clause if there is a recognized hazard of workplace violence in their establishments, and they do nothing to prevent or abate it. These standards address employee safety and security risks.

In September of 2011 OSHA announced a new directive targeting workplace violence prevention. In this directive, OSHA is actively investigating and citing employers for failure to keep their workplace safe from threats and incidents of workplace violence. Some states have sought legislative solutions, including mandatory establishment of a comprehensive prevention program for employers and employees.

If you are reading this book and have not gone through AVADE® Workplace Violence Prevention Training, ask your employer if they have adopted policies and procedures and response training for preventing workplace violence. If not, request to have AVADE® training.

At the very least, read and re-read this book. Ultimately, your safety is YOUR responsibility, but your employer may simply not know what's available as training for you and your co-workers.

Crime and Violence in the Workplace

Violence in the workplace is commonly understood as any physical assault, emotional or verbal abuse, or threatening, harassing, or coercive behavior in the work setting that causes physical or emotional harm.

Workplace Violence Statistics

- Almost 2 million employees suffer non-fatal workplace assaults.
- Homicide is the fourth-leading cause of fatal occupational injury in the US.
- Homicide is the leading cause of workplace death for females.
- Most non-fatal workplace assaults occur in the service industry, typically by the guest/client.
- Bureau of Labor Statistics: 50% of non-fatal injuries to workers from assaults and violent acts occur in social service settings.

Workplace Shootings

The US Bureau of Labor and Statistic on Workplace Shootings:
- From 2006-2010, 551 work-related homicides occurred each year in the US.
- 77 of these incidents were multiple-fatality homicide incidents (2 or more workers killed).
- Shootings accounted for 78 percent of all homicides in 2010 (405 fatal injuries).
- Robbers accounted for 72% of homicides to men and 37% to women.
- Nearly half of the shootings (48 percent) occurred in public buildings.
- Most shootings occurred in the private sector (83 percent).
- 17 percent of shootings occurred in government.
- Assailants with no known personal relationship to their victims accounted for about two-thirds of workplace homicides

Workplace violence can be devastating to deal with. If you have suffered from a violent incident, you may need to seek some type of assistance (Employee Assistance Program). Learning and integrating the **AVADE® techniques** in the training course and in this book will help ensure that you know what to look for. This will reduce the chances of YOU becoming a victim of workplace violence.

Crime and Violence in Healthcare

Emergency Nurses Association (ENA) study of Workplace Violence against Registered Nurses: The **ENA** defined **WPV** as any act of aggression directed toward persons at work or on duty that ranges from offensive or threatening to homicide. Workplace violence is commonly understood as any physical assault, emotional or verbal abuse, or threatening, harassing, or coercive behavior in the work setting that causes physical or emotional harm.

WPV Statistics

- Almost 2 million employees suffer non-fatal workplace assaults.
- Homicide leading cause of workplace death for females.
- Most non-fatal workplace assaults occur in the service industry, typically by the customer/patient.
- Costs of non-fatal workplace assaults: 876,000 lost work days per year - $16 million in lost wages per year.
- Bureau of Labor Statistics—50% of non-fatal injuries to workers from assaults and violent acts occur in healthcare or social service settings.
- Healthcare industry: leads all other sectors in the incidence of non-fatal workplace assaults at a rate of nearly four times that of the overall private sector injury rate.

ENA (Emergency Nurses Association) Emergency Department Violence Surveillance Study –November 2011

- Frequency of physical violence and verbal abuse during a seven-day period was reported by almost 55% of Emergency Dept. Nurses surveyed.
- Participants reported experiencing physical violence (with/without verbal abuse) (12.1%) and verbal abuse only (42.5%) during the survey period.
- The majority of the participants who were victims of workplace violence did not file a formal incident/event report for the physical violence or the verbal abuse.
- The presence of reporting policies (especially zero-tolerance policies), was associated with a lower odds of physical violence and verbal abuse.
- **Nurses whose hospital administration and ED management are committed to workplace violence control are less likely to experience workplace violence.**

AVADE® is based on Extensive Research

AVADE® WPV Prevention Training is based on research from OSHA, FBI, ASIS, IAHSS, CDC, NIOSH, SHRM, BLS, State WPV Laws, Department of Labor & Industries, the Dept. of Justice and more...

A comprehensive look at the **AVADE® Training's** research can be found in the bibliography in the back of this student manual.

The AVADE® Philosophy:

The Principles in the AVADE® Training Programs stand for:

A = Awareness
V = Vigilance
A = Avoidance
D = Defense
E = Escape/Environment

The **AVADE® philosophy** incorporates learning new habits, skills and actions that employers and employees can use to enhance their personal safety and their ability to defend themselves or others from dangerous situations, crime and violence.

AVADE® has been taught in private corporations, healthcare agencies, schools, community programs, and civic institutions for many years. The founder of the AVADE® Training programs, David Fowler, has over thirty years' experience and has made personal safety training his life's work. He has an extensive background in training, martial science, and all functions of security management and operations. He is also the author of *Be Safe Not Sorry: The Art and Science of Keeping You and Your Family Safe from Crime and Violence*, available on amazon.com and at his websites:

www.personalsafetytraining.com and **www.avadetraining.com.**

> **"The overall vision and philosophy of the AVADE® Training program is the moral essence of life itself: to live a safe and positive life with peace, security, harmony and freedom of choice."**

The AVADE® Workplace Violence Prevention system is designed to give you the training and education you'll need in the prevention and mitigation of violence in the workplace. Agencies must also consider and implement the appropriate administrative, behavioral and environmental categories for developing protocols and procedures for their workplace violence prevention plan.

AVADE® Workplace Modules and Objectives

AVADE® Training is a modular-based training program which can be taught in:
E-Learning - Employee orientation - Two hour sessions - Four hour sessions - Eight hour sessions - Two day sessions - Or presented during safety or departmental meetings throughout a 12-month period. - Or modular training combining classroom, self-defense and defensive control tactics—8+ hrs.

AVADE® Workplace Violence Prevention Modules & Objectives: AVADE® principles and learning objectives are integrated throughout the Administrative, Behavioral, and Environmental components of an effective Workplace Violence Prevention Plan.

1. **Awareness:** Your Workplace Violence Prevention Plan will increase your overall awareness of worker risks to violence, and provide strategies to prevent and mitigate these risks.

2. **Vigilance:** Understanding the characteristics of violence and the predicting factors related to it.

3. **Avoidance:** Reduce and eliminate incidents of workplace violence through administrative, behavioral and environmental protocols and procedures.

4. **Interpersonal Communications:** Understanding the assault cycle and developing skills to de-escalate the different types of aggressive behaviors are important factors in mitigating workplace violence.

5. **Defense of Self and Others:** Mitigate liability risk through proper documentation and the understanding of using force to defend ones-self or others.

6. **Stress Management:** Provide methods of team debriefing, post-incident response and techniques for dealing with daily stressors.

7. **Time & Distance:** Increase understanding of reactionary response to a physical or weapon assault situation.

8. **Escape Planning:** Pre-planning escape routes from all environments and learning physical maneuvers and positioning to prevent isolation and assaultive situations.

9. **Environmental Factors:** Understand appropriate safety techniques and departmental systems and procedures for the different areas of the workplace.

10. **Emergency Codes and Procedures:** Provide and increase awareness of the agencies protocols and procedures for responding to an emergent situation.

The AVADE Training program is incorporated into three training levels:

Level I – Education, Prevention and Mitigation of Workplace Violence
Level II – Self-Defense Tactics and Techniques
Level III – Defensive Control Tactics and Techniques

AVADE® Level II Self-Defense Tactics

- The Goal of Self-Defense
- Fundamentals of Self-Defense
- Defensive Blocking Techniques
- PDW's (Personal Defensive Weapons)
- Defense from Physical Assaults (Frontal)
- Defense from Physical Assaults (Rear)
- Use of Force and Documentation

AVADE® Level III Defensive Control Tactics

- Introduction to Defensive Control
- Fundamentals of Defensive Control
- Contact and Cover Positioning
- Escort Strategies and Techniques
- Control and Decentralization Techniques
- Prone and Supine Control Techniques
- * Healthcare Restraint Techniques
- Use of Force and Documentation

The **AVADE® Workplace Violence Prevention** Training program will teach you how to recognize emerging situations, how to deal with someone before they become violent, and how to survive and escape a violent attack and much, much more. Read carefully. Integrate the lessons you learn here. Unfortunately, one day you may be responsible for saving your own life—and the lives of your co-workers.

Chapter 1: Creating an Effective Workplace Violence Prevention Plan

The Three Categories of an Effective Workplace Violence Prevention Plan

1. Administrative   2. Behavioural   3. Environmental

There are many components to the administrative policies, practices and procedures for a successful Workplace Violence Prevention system:

Administrative Protocols and Procedures

Workplace Violence Prevention Policy: The importance of a comprehensive policy that strictly prohibits violence and threats against the workplace, as well as other behaviors deemed inappropriate is the foundation of preventing violence in the workplace.

No reprisal reporting policy: It's vital to create an atmosphere where employees feel safe reporting strange, threatening or abusive behavior. If employees fear reprisal, people in authority may never know that an employee, client or guest is behaving in a threatening manner. Some employers have instituted anonymous caller lines, where employees can leave information and keep their anonymity.

Documentation and record keeping: Documentation is essential in reducing the liability an agency could be exposed to. If an employee needs to be let go, or a client or guest needs to be barred from the premises, documentation of inappropriate behavior will be necessary for legal purposes. Proper documentation also allows companies to mitigate certain areas that have been identified through tracking and trending.

Incident reporting procedures/structures: Many states require that all workplace incidents/injuries be reported to the Department of Labor and Industries or other regulatory agencies. Proper reporting structures must be in place for managers and supervisors. Employees need to be trained to identify and report incidents that could be indicative of an emerging problem.

Security management prevention plan: A security management plan helps employers identify risk factors and risk areas. Once identified a well-trained security manager and team can respond to, and more importantly, prevent situations from escalating to violence. This proactive response planning identifies potential risk factors with strategies to prevent, reduce and eliminate risks to staff, clients and guests.

Management commitment and employee involvement: AVADE® training has many components. From basic employee awareness training to more advanced training. We recognize that security, management, supervisors, human resources personnel and department directors play a unique role in workplace violence prevention and will need more tools. Using the **AVADE®** training and principles, everyone in an organization can participate in keeping the workplace safe. Overall, to successfully prevent and mitigate workplace violence the commitment must come from the top down. It's essential to get leadership buy-in.

Emergency code procedures and response: Chapter 12 discusses some common emergent situations that happen in all industries. Things as simple as knowing where your exits are, knowing how to dial 911 out from a company line, and knowing where alarm buttons are can save lives. Proper training in emergency codes and response is critical.

Departmental risk level assessment: Certain risk factors help us identify if a department is a low, medium or high risk. Department managers must also have the training to identify potentially dangerous situations, and know the procedures for responding to and reporting them. Many companies utilize the security management plan to help identify risk factors in all departments and work areas.

Workplace Violence Program evaluation: Knowing that workplace violence is a three-pronged process: *administrative, behavioral, environmental.* An employer's overall program should be reviewed periodically to ensure its effectiveness. As the environment changes in the workplace, so will the plan needed to reduce potential risks.

Human Resources: HR plays an integral role in the development and implementation of a successful workplace violence prevention, mitigation and intervention planning. Policy development, staff training, incident tracking and reporting, union negotiations, departmental coordination efforts and disciplinary actions to enforce policies are key components in which human resources involvement is necessary.

Human Resources hiring and termination protocols and procedures: With consistent, careful pre-employment background checks, many problems can be averted. Termination procedures should be handled correctly and consistently by trained individuals who understand the potential risk factors and warning signs of workplace violence.

Legal Counsel: Using in-house or an outside firm for an understanding of the legal obligations related to workplace violence is essential to an organization.

Threat Assessment Team: A threat assessment team is a group of individuals, usually comprised of security management, human resources, department heads, administration and others. This team evaluates the risk factors of an individual with warning signs who has been recently disciplined, terminated or is being investigated for workplace violence. The team collaborates and determines best course of action. During high-risk assessments, a clinical psychologist specializing in workplace violence may need to be retained from an established reputable consulting firm.

Staffing levels: Particularly in retail and health care settings, it's vital that sufficient personnel are present for the safety of employees. The old saying holds true, "there is safety in numbers."

Behavioral Training

Training and Education: AVADE® Workplace Violence Prevention training is perhaps the most important component in a **Workplace Violence Prevention Program**. Understanding risk factors and what constitutes potentially dangerous behavior—and how to deal with it—is the first line of defense against workplace violence.

Post Incident response procedures: If a workplace violence incident DOES occur, policies and procedures need to be in place beforehand so that employees have a clear course of action and know what to do. See Chapter 8 for information on how to respond after an incident has occurred.

Post incident reporting procedures: For legal protection of yourself, your co-workers, and your company, proper post-incident reporting is essential. Post follow up to incidents can help reduce and even eliminate re-occurrence if action steps are taken.

Self-Defense and appropriate Use of Force: We all have the right to defend ourselves. Proper training and education in self-defense techniques, and an understanding of the appropriate use of force has reduced injury, saved lives and reduced liability exposure. Certain industries will need comprehensive training on controlling and restraining individuals. Healthcare, security, law enforcement and behavioral health typically need additional training in this category, as their jobs are at higher risk.

Environmental

Creating a physically safe environment for employees has been shown to minimize threats to employees, guests and clients/customers. Rather than industrial concerns (such as ensuring heavy equipment is save to use), here we're talking about environmental components that promote and support the **Workplace Violence Prevention Program.** See Chapter 11 for information on the environmental tools in your environments that can help keep you safe.

Worksite audit/analysis: Similar to a security management plan but specific to all areas of the workplace and anywhere employees are. Many employers use audits and analysis of workplace violence incidents to help identify, prevent and mitigate risk. An environmental analysis would include checking in areas outside of a workplace, where someone could hide out in shrubbery etc.

Panic alarms: Proper placement for high-risk areas and staff education on using them are essential. Do you know where your panic alarms are? Do you even have panic alarms? If so, do you know how to use them and what happens after they have been activated?

Access controls: Door locks and security devices on doors are designed to keep people out and are only good when employees and staff use them properly. Doors propped open, piggy backing, and access numbers written above the lock fail to ensure a safe work area.

Physical Lighting: Criminals don't like lights! Things as simple as ensuring there are no broken/unusable lights in bathrooms, dark hallways and parking lots can keep people safe from a violent incident and reduce crime.

CPTED = Crime Prevention through Environmental Design: This concept is gaining ground around the world. CPTED promotes things such as lighting, ensuring pedestrian routes are open and visible, even minimizing shrubbery in vulnerable places so that assailants have no place to hide. Many corporations utilize CPTED in pre-design and new construction. It can also be utilized in environmental security audits and analysis as well as the security management plan.

Proactive Response Planning = Prevention and Intervention

Proactive vs. Reactive: Prevention and intervention are essential to eliminating and mitigating security risks in the workplace. Employers now recognize the importance of being proactive in their implementation of workplace violence policies and procedures, conducting work site audits/analysis, tracking and trending incidents, training and educating staff, as well as other proactive measures to reduce the risk of violence to guests, staff, clients and visitors. A well-thought-out plan for the prevention of workplace violence takes on a proactive response versus an after-the-fact, reactive-driven response.

_____

_____

_____

_____

_____

_____

_____

_____

_____

_____

_____

_____

_____

_____

_____

_____

_____

Chapter 2

Personal Safety Measures and Habits

Whose responsibility is your Personal Safety?

General Personal Safety Measures

MIND, BODY, SPIRIT and ENVIRONMENT—General personal safety measures involve maintaining a balance and awareness in all areas of your life: mental, physical, spiritual and your environments.

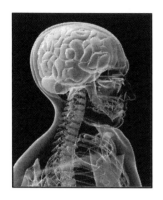 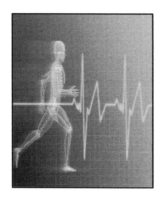 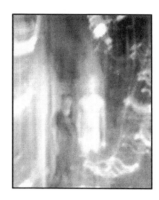 

Personal Safety & Self-Defense Habits*: What is a Habit?*

> *"We are what we repeatedly do; therefore, excellence is not an act, it is a habit."* - Aristotle, Greek Philosopher

Habits are our acquired patterns of behavior that occur automatically without thought, things we repeatedly do over and over. They can be either good or bad.

We Are Creatures of Habit

You get up in the morning a certain way and get ready for your day. You brush your teeth; comb your hair, put on your clothes, etc., the same way, every day. You don't even think about it, you just do it. The way you answer the phone, greet people, shake hands, gesture, smile or not smile are also all your habits. Habits are ingrained in you and stamped into your unconscious mind.

Habits are powerful factors in our lives. They are consistent, unconscious patterns that constantly and daily express our character and produce our effectiveness…or ineffectiveness. Habits determine your future and your safety!

> **"Sow an act and you reap a habit. Sow a habit and you reap a character. Sow a character and you reap a destiny."**
>
> -Charles Reade, English Novelist, (1814-1884)

General Personal Safety Measures involve maintaining a balance in all areas of one's life. The four areas of your Personal Safety involve mental, physical, spiritual and environmental understanding, awareness, ability and understanding.

How do you rate your personal safety habits? _____

Developing Personal Safety Habits

- **Identify Limiting Habits**
- **Let's play "21"**
- **Creating New Habits**
- **Taking Action (visualize)**
- **No Retreat, No Surrender Policy**
- **Evaluate Yourself**
- **Benefits and Commitment**

Habits = Automatic Responses

A Habit is something that we repeatedly do over and over, an acquired pattern or behavior that occurs automatically without thought.

Identify Your Limiting Personal Safety Habits: Do you have habits that leave you unsafe? Such as leaving your car unlocked, or working late and cutting through unlit areas? Take a hard look at your daily habits and see what little things you can do to ensure your own safety. Once identified, you can begin to change and improve them.

The 21 Rule: This is the process of making small adjustments in your behavior. Twenty-one days of repeatedly doing what you intend to do, to create a new habit. The 21 Rule is not applicable to a habit that we have had for an extended time. Long-term habits have roots like trees and run very deep. Changing or eliminating long-term habits could take as long as a year or more to develop or break.

Creating New Habits: Write out your new personal safety habits. Once you identify your limiting and successful habits, you can clearly decide to change them, or make new, more productive and empowering personal safety habits. Having a clear, defined personal safety goal is the first powerful step to creating a new habit.

Take Action with <u>Visualization</u>: Written words are powerful—but only when you look at them, and make an effort and a commitment to follow through. Focus on your new personal safety habits often; focus on the benefits of your new habits. Use the process of visualization to add more repetitions to your successful new habit. More on this in section on Awareness; using mental movies.

The No Retreat, No Surrender Policy: The no-surrender policy means that you will do whatever it takes to change or accomplish your personal safety goal. This policy is about doing it even when you don't feel like it—when you're tired, sick, hungry or stressed. You do it no matter what; you make the commitment!

Evaluate Yourself and Ask for Help: Ask yourself, could I do more to improve my general personal safety and overall sense of safety? Ask for help and get more training. A good trainer will gladly let you know the areas that you could improve upon. Look to improve in all the areas that you received negative feedback, too. Negative feedback is not necessarily "bad." Consider negative feedback as a way to add safety and self-improvement to your personal life. It's about taking responsibility for yourself and your circumstances.

Commitment Exercise

COMMITMENT	EXERCISE
If you change or add one new, empowering habit every other month, in five years you will have thirty new habits. Remember, habits are something we unconsciously do; once they're ingrained, you don't even have to think about them.	Commit to developing at least one habit for each workplace violence prevention module. Write it down in your **AVADE® Workplace Violence Prevention Manual.** Focus on it often

Habits are ingrained in you and stamped into your unconscious mind.

Developing Personal Safety Habits

Ask yourself, could I do more to improve my general personal safety and overall sense of safety? Ask for help and get more training. A good trainer will gladly let you know the areas that you could improve upon. Look to improve in all the areas that you received negative feedback too. Negative feedback is not necessarily "bad". Consider negative feedback as a way to add safety and self-improvement to your personal life. It's about taking responsibility for yourself and your circumstances.

Benefits of AVADE® Workplace Violence Prevention Training

- Increased Awareness
- Increased Confidence
- Increased Overall Safety
- Increased Quality of Life
- Increased Self-Improvement
- Increased Sense of Overall Peace
- Increased Ability to Protect Others

You will also experience:

- Reduced Fear
- Reduced Stress
- Reduced Injuries
- Reduced Liability Risk
- Reduced Loss of Property
- Reduced Feelings of Inadequacy
- Reduced Inability to Respond to Situations

After going through an **AVADE® Workplace Violence Prevention Training Program**, refer back to this textbook "AVADE® Workplace Violence Prevention" as your personal refresher course.

The textbook on workplace violence prevention will help remind you how to recognize emerging situations, how to deal with someone before they become violent, and how to survive and escape a violent attack and much-much more. **Read and study carefully**. Integrate the lessons you learn here. Unfortunately, one day you may be responsible for saving your own life—and the lives of your co-workers.

Chapter 3: Increase Your Awareness

Awareness Defined

Everything in life begins with **Awareness**. Have you ever said this to yourself: "I would have done that if I had been of aware it." The goal of this chapter is to help you understand what awareness is and how you can increase yours. There are many levels of awareness and we will briefly look at them and why they are important to your safety in the workplace.

Awareness is defined as: *A mental state or ability to perceive, feel or be conscious of people, emotions, conditions, events, objects, and patterns.*

- The key to awareness is knowledge and understanding.
- The gift of this awareness is wisdom.
- Change your awareness and you can change your life!

> "Every human has four endowments- self-awareness, conscience, independent will and creative imagination. These give us the ultimate human freedom... the power to choose, to respond, to change."
>
> -Stephen R. Covey, *The 7 Habits of Highly Effective People*

Increase your Awareness of Worker Risks to Workplace Violence

- **Lack of staff training in recognition and de-escalation of workplace risks:** The biggest risk is not recognizing that an individual is escalating and not knowing how to avoid the situation or how to use your interpersonal communication skills to de-escalate that person.

- **Working alone or in isolated areas:** When working alone, remember to increase your 360 view of awareness to keep yourself safe. Practice what police officers do when dealing with a person in conflict, get back-up!

- **Not using or having electronic safety measures:** Electronic safety measures (alarms, access controls etc.) are only as good as the people using them. Unrestricted movement of the public can put workers at risk. Know and understand how the safety controls in your environment work. If not sure, as questions—get training.

- **Contact with prisoners and the mentally ill:** Some industries have a higher prevalence of contact with these individuals. However, any of us can be exposed to mentally ill consumers and ex-inmates. Be aware and have a plan.

- **Low staffing levels and increased consumer waiting:** It's a fact of life in our current economy; we are all expected to do more with less. This means our consumers may have to wait for our services or products. Mealtimes, visiting hours and overcrowded-uncomfortable waiting rooms may precipitate the risk. Use interpersonal communication skills when dealing with consumers who are upset.

- **An increase and prevalence of weapons in society:** Weapons are everywhere; they can be everyday common tools we use at work. Increase you awareness of what is around you and how it may be used as a weapon to inflict harm.
  Guns and knives are not the only threat we face today.

- **Presence of gang members and high crime areas:** Demographics of where we live, commute and work are factors that predispose us to crime and violence. Be aware of these potential areas of risk and avoid if possible.

- **Access to pharmaceuticals/drug seekers:** One thing is for certain, people will continue to seek and use drugs. Working with pharmaceuticals can put you at risk. Increased awareness is needed for industries that prescribe or administer drugs.

- **Drug and alcohol use among consumers:** Working with people who are under the influence of alcohol or prescribed and non-prescribed drugs may expose a person to an increased risk.

- **Distraught family members and visitors:** Stressed individuals may escalate into higher levels of the assault cycle. Recognizing that a person is distraught can increase your ability to de-escalate them.

- **Handling of money/transactions:** Anytime you work with valuables or money there is an increase in risk. Assaults and robberies take place daily due to the fact that certain individuals will commit crimes to get those assets.

- **Public Access (often 24/7):** Any workplace that is open to the public around the clock exposes employees to certain risks. An increase of criminal behavior occurs more often during certain times of the day than at others times.

- **Late and early work hours:** When workers arrive or leave work during late night or early hours it may expose them to an increased risk of workplace violence. Workers are encouraged to get security escorts if available and travel to and from parking areas with co-workers.

- **Home care visits:** Entering into another person's residence may leave a person vulnerable. Certain precautions and training should take place to equip personnel on what to look for and how to respond when providing home care visits.

- **History of Violence and inadequate Security and Mental Health personnel on site:** Working with individuals who have a history of violence predisposes staff to risk. This risk is increased if Security and Mental Health personnel are not available to deal with individuals with violent behaviors. Appropriate training and mental preparation prepares staff for increased risk factors.

- **Transporting Patients and Clients:** Individuals who transport patient and clients should be vigilant as they are often alone and in multiple environments. Stay Aware!

- **Poor Environmental Design:** Poorly lit corridors, parking lots, or other areas where objects block employee's vision. Stay vigilant and use your environmental awareness.

- **Lack of Emergency Communication:** Without procedures and tools to communicate for help, workers are affected as emergent response is delayed or absent. Panic alarms, cell phones, blue phones, radios, paging and other methods of communication should be utilized if available. Training for emergency codes and procedures; see chapter 12.

- **Perception that Violence is Tolerated:** A perception that victims will not or cannot report the incident to police and press charges is a precipitating factor which often leads to more acts of violence on staff. A NO tolerance policy for violence should be established and enforced. Violence will NOT be tolerated!

_____

_____

_____

_____

_____

_____

_____

_____

_____

_____

Levels of Awareness:

- **Self-Awareness**
- **Emotional Awareness**
- **Situational Awareness**
- **Environmental Awareness**
- **Unconscious Awareness**
- **Higher Awareness**

Self-Awareness:

This conscious awareness allows you to think, reason, choose and exercise free will, evaluate options and make decisions. Through your self-awareness you have communication with your body through the sensations of sight, sound, smell, taste and touch. You are using your self-awareness right now as you look at these words, decipher the meaning, think about the message and make decisions of its validity.

Emotional Awareness:

Your ability to recognize and feel the emotions and feelings of others, as well as your own, is your emotional awareness.

When you are aware and in control of your emotions you can communicate with compassion and empathy. When you are emotionally aware, you also recognize the patterns and changes in others around you. This ability to know that a co-worker or regular client's behaviors have changed can give you the opportunity to intervene, report your concerns or distance yourself from the individual.

Emotions are "the glue" connecting people to one another. They are the foundation of our ability to understand ourselves and relate to others. When you are aware and in control of your emotions, you can think clearly and creatively; manage stress and challenges; communicate well with others; and display trust, empathy, compassion and confidence.

When we lose control of our emotions, we spin into confusion, isolation, and doubt. By learning to recognize, manage, and deal with your emotions, you'll enjoy greater happiness, health and better relationships.

Your emotions help you:

- Understand yourself, including your deeply-felt needs

- Understand and empathize with others

- Communicate clearly and effectively

- Make decisions based on the things that are most important to you

- Get motivated and take action to meet goals

- Build strong, healthy relationships

Understanding the emotions in others as well as yourself helps you evaluate the behaviors of others and how you are feeling about a person's behaviors. How does all this relate to your safety in the workplace? Simple: trust your feelings/emotions. If a situation or someone in particular is raising your level of fear or anxiety, trust that feeling and take the appropriate actions.

Situational Awareness:

Situational awareness means being aware of what is happening around you. It means understanding how information, incidents, and your own actions will affect your goals and objectives, both now and in the near future. Lacking situational awareness or having inadequate situational awareness has been identified as one of the primary factors in accidents attributed to human error.

It is best explained in a simple equation: I_____ + R_____ = O_____
If an individual is angry and escalating (*incident*) and knowing how to respond (*response*) to the situation can lead to a non-violent *outcome*. By taking responsibility for all the situations you are in, you can increase your personal safety, by making conscious, informed choices and decisions about your environments, the people around you, and the places you frequent.

Environmental Awareness:

Environmental awareness is the ability to understand and recognize the many factors relating to your environment and how they can benefit you or limit you.

It also means having: **An understanding that your external physical conditions can affect and influence your growth, development, and physical survival.**

Creating an awareness of what is around you at all times is described as a 360-degree environmental awareness.

Unconscious Awareness:

Unconscious awareness is the part of the mind that directs the involuntary and automatic processes of the body. Through its operation, it automatically rebuilds, repairs and operates your body.

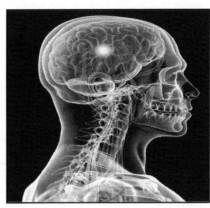

Your **unconscious awareness is the storehouse of your memory, habits, beliefs, instincts, emotions and knowledge.**

In chapter 2 we discussed the importance of personal safety habits. Knowing that habits reside in this part of our awareness gives us the opportunity to program our automatic responses by using the mental movie techniques to create personal safety habits.

"He who fails to plan, plans to fail"

Mental Movies and Impressing the Unconscious Mind

As humans we have the ability to pre-play events in our mind. We also have the ability to re-play past events in our mind. Most people have experienced both facets of playing mental movies and impressing the non-conscious mind. Unfortunately, most people spend far more energy pre-playing negative events (worry) and re-playing negative events (past events that were negative) than visualizing positive outcomes

Make a conscious choice to pre-play events to your liking and re-play positive events.
Here is how we impress the unconscious mind so that we can respond automatically without having to stop and think about what we need to do. A preplanned response can literally save your life.

Stage 1: Create the scene of the event, incident or situation in your mind's eye.

Stage 2: Make the scene as clear and colorful as possible. Focus your mind's eye as you create this clear concise mental scene.

Stage 3: "Lights, Focus, Camera and Action!" Now that the scene is clear and focused, give it action. As the director of your mental movie you direct everything in it.

Stage 4: The plot/outcome is up to you! You decide what happens, when it happens and who it happens to. You are the hero of your mental movie. You always win in your mind's eye when you create, direct and choreograph the mental movie.

Stage 5: Feel what it is like to be the star of your mental movie. Positive energy helps build, reinforce and utilize the mental power we all have. This ultimately makes us stronger, more decisive and automatic in our responses.

Stage 6: Remember to pre-play your mental movie prior to situations happening. We are the only creature with this ability. Re-play positive outcomes and try not to re-play negative outcomes of real situations. If you do re-play negative situations in your mind's eye make sure to always change the outcome to your choosing.

The Amazing Mind

The Human Mind is the most complex and powerful machine in the universe. Properly preparing your mind through mental movie exercises is one of the most important aspects of violence intervention. Your physical body's performance is increased through mental training.

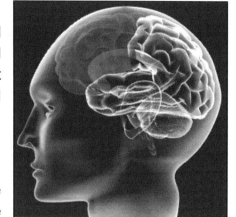

Higher Awareness:

Many, if not most, people believe in some form of an infinite and eternal energy from which all things proceed. It is the reality that underlies all existence and is everywhere present. This state of awareness is the highest, as it encompasses all the levels of your awareness as well as your spiritual/energetic awareness. Some people call this awareness a sixth sense, and many people have credited it with keeping them out of dangerous situations, or even saving their lives.

Constant Communication

Our self-awareness, emotional awareness, situational awareness, environmental awareness, unconscious awareness and higher awareness are in a constant state of communication with each other. Even though we are not cognizant of this, it is continuously present. Just knowing this is the beginning of increased awareness.

Developing & Increasing Awareness

Developing and increasing your awareness does not mean becoming paranoid or hyper-vigilant. It simply means using all your senses

Improve and Increase your Awareness
There are several ways to improve and increase your awareness.

1. Planning and preparing for situations that haven't happened yet. This is done by pre-playing (mental movies) what you would do if faced with a crisis situation.

2. Being Responsible or **"Response-able"** is the ability to choose your awareness, responses and attitude towards incidents, yourself and others.

3. Pay Attention to what is going on inside of you and outside of you.

4. Be Present. You don't have to keep your mind constantly busy thinking about all the possible things that can go amiss. Be present or in the moment allows your awareness to be at its most optimal state.

5. Be Proactive. Recognize the importance of responsibility and awareness. Proactive people don't blame circumstances or conditions for their behavior or outcomes. Their behavior and outcomes are a product of their own conscious choices, based on their knowledge and values rather than their circumstances.

6. Attitude Is Everything. Your success with everything you do depends on your attitude. Creating a positive attitude about life and all of the events you will experience will help develop and enhance your awareness.

Make small commitments and keep them.
Be a light, not a judge. Be a model, not a critic.
Be part of the solution, not part of the problem.

_____

_____

_____

_____

_____

_____

Chapter 4: Vigilance

What is Vigilance?

Vigilance is the <u>practice</u> of paying attention to our internal and external messages with regards to ourselves, other people, things and events.

"We can never relax our vigilance about crime, about enforcement, about prevention... there's going to be some new problem down the road."

- Janet Reno, the first woman Attorney General of the U.S.

Hypervigilance

NOTE: Hypervigilance is a negative condition of maintaining an abnormal awareness of environmental stimuli that causes anxiety, leads to exhaustion and causes us to startle easily.

Hypervigilance is counter-productive and unhealthy. Learning the AVADE® principles will give you the tools you need to live a happy, safe life without allowing fear to consume you.

All great men are gifted with intuition. They know without reasoning or analysis, what they need to know."

- Alexis Carrel, French Biologist and Noble Prize Winner, 1912

The Five Senses: Touch, smell, hearing, taste and sight, are the mental connection through our bodies to the outer world. Our senses can also alert us and keep us safe from danger. Many people believe that there is a sixth sense.

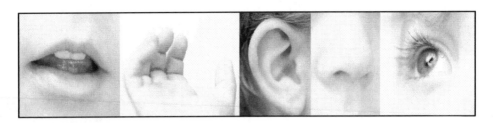

Is there a Sixth Sense?

Trust your intuition, your sixth sense. Intuition is knowing without knowing why. Intuition communicates with us through symbols, feelings, and emotions. It's like radar for sensing, seeing or feeling danger before it is present.

Intuition is a personal security system that is always on and ever vigilant, surveying not only danger, but everything else as well.

Trust your intuition!

Intuition is a process of gaining information that does not rely on your senses, memory, experiences, or thought processes.

"The intuitive mind is a sacred gift and the rational mind is a faithful servant. We have created a society that honors the servant and has forgotten the gift."
- Albert Einstein

Using Your Intuition

The ability to read a person's attitudes and thoughts by their behaviors was the original communication system used by humans prior to spoken language. In his book, *Body Talk: The Meaning of Human Gestures*, author Desmond Morris lists more than fifty body signals (messages) that are universal to all human beings in every culture. The majority of these messages are communicated unconsciously. Just as the communication is unconscious, so is our ability to read this non-verbal communication. If you were asked to identify just ten of the non-verbal messages, you may find it difficult, but we all know them and respond to them intuitively. The key to using your intuition more effectively is to bring the unconscious data it supplies to a place where your conscious mind can interpret it. Intuition is always communicating to you. Occasionally it may send a signal that turns out to be less than dangerous, but everything it communicates to you is meaningful.

Intuition might send any of several messengers to get your attention, and because they differ according to urgency, it is good to know the various messages.

Messages of Intuition:

Synchronicity: This is the message all of us get. It the connectedness we all have and write off as airy-fairy. The best example of this is a phone call. All of us have been thinking about that particular someone and the phone rings and it's them.

This happens to all of us in many ways every day.

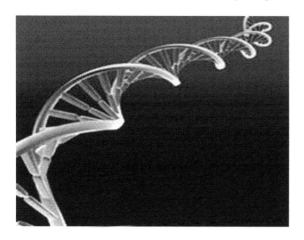

Messages of Intuition
- **Synchronicity**
- **Nagging Feelings**
- **Hunches**
- **Gut Feeling**
- **Hesitation/Doubt**
- **Suspicion**
- **Physical Changes**
- **Danger**

"If there is anything intuition demonstrates, it's the interconnectedness of everything."

- Carl Jung, Synchronicity

Synchronicity: This is the message all of us get. It the connectedness we all have and write off as airy-fairy. The best example of this is a phone call. All of us have been thinking about that particular someone and the phone rings and it's them. This happens to all of us in many ways every day.

Nagging Feelings: When we experience nagging feelings about someone or something it is our unconscious awareness telling us to wait and question what is going on.

Hunches: A hunch is a feeling that a particular event or situation will go a certain way.

Gut Feeling: A term many of us like to use in regard to predicting something that may or may not happen. For some of us a gut feeling is visceral; we can literally feel it.

Hesitation/Doubt: When we hesitate and doubt we are stalling for more time and questioning the situation.

Suspicion: For some, being suspicious is their internal radar that says "something isn't right here."

Physical Changes: Like other species, we too, change physically when exposed to internal and external intuitive messages. When the hair stands up on the back of your neck or when you get goose bumps, your body is telling you something.

Danger: The intuitive messenger with the greatest urgency is **DANGER**. When you know with all of your being that you are in trouble or a situation is imminent is the intuitive message of danger.

Developing Intuition

Learning to read body language teaches us to be more sensitive to people's feelings and emotions, provide better customer service or care to those who rely on us, and increase our personal safety.

Developing your intuitive ability begins with paying attention to what's going on inside of you so that you can become aware of these inner signals and catch them when they are happening, or shortly afterward.

NOTE: The enemy of intuition is worry. When you play or replay negative situations, spending energy on things that have already happened or might happen soon, you don't have the mental space to acknowledge and act on signals your intuition is trying to send to you!

Stop-Look-Listen
Developing and using your intuition means you need to stop, look and listen occasionally to what your feelings, senses, perceptions and contexts of situations are telling you at that present moment.

Listening to, trusting, and acting on your intuitive inner guidance is an art. And like any art or discipline, it requires an ongoing commitment. Challenge yourself to develop a deeper understanding of self-awareness.

"They that are on their guard and appear ready to receive their adversaries are in much less danger of being attacked than the supine, secure and negligent."

– Benjamin Franklin, one of the founding fathers of the USA

Chapter 5: Avoidance

"The best self-defense is to not be there when the attack takes place."
– David Fowler, author of *Be Safe Not Sorry*
and *Violence in the Workplace*

Who commits violence? People do! The types of individuals who commit violence are categorized into five areas: stranger violence, guest/client violence, lateral violence, domestic violence, and extreme violence.

There are specific characteristics for all five types of individual violence listed below. After examining these characteristics, we will look at strategies to prevent, mitigate or eliminate your risk of violence from these individuals.

Stranger	Client/Patient	Lateral	Domestic	Extreme

Stranger Violence Includes:

- Rape
- Robbery
- Assaults (verbal and physical)
- Bomb threats
- Gang violence

- **Homicide: occurs when one human being causes the death of another human being.**
- **Homicides can be divided into types: murder, manslaughter, justifiable etc...**

Stranger violence also includes verbal threats, threatening behavior or physical assaults by an assailant who has no legitimate business or relationship to the workplace. This person may enter the workplace to commit a criminal act or robbery. In most states, violence by strangers accounts for most of the fatalities related to workplace violence.

Stranger violence occurs between offenders and victims who have no prior relationship. Unlike crimes that take place between family members, friends, business partners, or acquaintances, stranger violence occurs when the offender is not known to the victim in any way. Violent crime refers to crimes including, but not limited to, homicide, sexual assault, assault, robbery, and other violent offenses. While most violent crimes are perpetrated by offenders known to the victims, violence between strangers is still thought of as one of the most frightening forms of violence.

Robbery Prevention and Response (see Robbery Code –Chapter 12)

Stranger Violence = Predator

What is a Predator?

1. An organism that lives by preying on other organisms.

2. One that victimizes, plunders, or destroys, especially for one's own gain.

A correlation can be made between predators in the wild and human predators in our society. A number of similarities are resent with both animals and humans.

> *Human Predators Want Three (3) Things*
> 1) *Valuables (money, assets, possessions etc...)*
> 2) *Bodies (physical / sexual assault –rape)*
> 3) *Lives (homicide-murder)*

Fortunately we and other (species) have learned to adapt (adaptation) and overcome against predators.

Predator-Prey and Adaptation

Adaptation is a basic phenomenon of biology, and also refers to characteristics which are especially important to an organism's survival.

Adaptive traits can be structural, behavioral, psychological and physiological.

- **Structural:** We as humans secure our homes, cars, and workplaces with locks, solid doors/window and use security devices, etc., to keep us safe.
- **Behavioral:** We have the ability to recognize threatening behaviors in others, as well as behave in ways as to not cause unwanted attention or portray ourselves as easy targets.
- **Psychological:** It all starts with having a mindset of awareness and vigilance.
- **Physiological:** Is self-awareness of our physical ability to use our senses and even be able to run, defend and take action if needed.

Predator and Prey:

A predator may be larger than its prey, stronger and sometimes faster. Predators develop their senses and always seek opportune times to strike. They will camouflage themselves using their environment and behaviors. And a predator is not always specific in regards to its prey, often it will seek more than one prey or type of prey. Most crime and violence occur during evening and nighttime hours. But, be cautious, as some predators will choose daytime to prey upon their victims as well.

The predator doesn't want someone who will resist, so he or she will select prey that is older, weaker, or very young. The predator's prey can be either male or female. The predator knows that a person's presence sends a message about their confidence and ability; people who are unaware become easy prey for predators. People who stand out or call unnecessary attention to themselves are advertising themselves as prey. Those who are distracted can also be victimized. And isolation gives the predator protection from unwanted attention.

The Reverse Line-Up

A typical police line-up is done with the suspects being lined up and the victim determining if any of the suspects in the line-up is the perpetrator of the crime. The reverse line-up is everyday people in everyday life, and the predator determines the prey he/she will select from that line-up. In a reverse line up, predators are evaluating and selecting their prey from a pool of potential victims: Us.

Predator Characteristics

(A characteristic is an attribute or trait of an entity with many particular meanings.)

- **Size**
- **Speed**
- **Senses**
- **Opportunist**
- **Camouflage**
- **Environment**
- **Not Specific**
- **Night and Day**

Intentions are a reflection of a person's thoughts coming from their face, body, posture, position of hands and their dress. Intentions can also show an individual's level of confidence, emotional state, and their motives and attitudes. **Pay attention to intentions!**

Don't Be Easy Prey: Don't be a victim. Don't be prey. Any of the mental states or what is known as **Prey Paradigms** listed below leave you vulnerable to observant predators. They'll know you're an easy target. Do not fall into this mental state—that's one of your best defenses for avoiding violence.

Un-Aware Unconsciously: An unconscious state of unawareness of a person's surroundings and the people they encounter. This unconscious state *is not knowing that you don't know.* But remember, ignorance is not a good defense.

Un-Prepared: A higher state of conscious awareness than being un-aware, but lacking in preparedness of potential situations. Have you ever said to yourself, "I'm just not that prepared for the day."

Un-Secured: Not using the precautionary security tools and equipment in a person's environments. Environmental components are in place to keep you safe. Not knowing where they are or how to use them is not a good defense.

Un-Aware Consciously: The most lacking in awareness is a dangerous state of denial—the "nothing can happen to me" mentality. It's when you just don't care and are consciously choosing to be unaware.

Un-Fortunate: Being in the wrong place at the wrong time. This paradigm mindset is the least likely event to happen; however, by increasing your awareness and your vigilance, you can lessen your chances of being in the wrong place at the wrong time.

Hard Target vs. Easy Target
Understanding the characteristics of individuals who commit violence, as well as what predators look for in their prey, increases your awareness and vigilance. And remember: if it doesn't feel right, it almost certainly isn't.

Prey (Victim) Characteristics

- Predators will always choose the easier target.
- Easy targets are easily identifiable.
- Predators will target easy prey and avoid prey that is harder or more of a risk for them.
- Having awareness and a presence that says "confidence" is the first step in avoiding a conflict with an assailant (predator).

Easy targets appear:

- **Un-Aware**
- **Distracted**
- **Have a non-confident presence**
- **Walk with a lackadaisical stride, with their eyes down, head down, and a slumped posture**
- **Use non-specific actions**
- **Have a timid or submissive presence**

Make yourself a Hard Target by:

Being aware: When it's obvious you are paying attention to what's around you, you are not an easy target.

Confident Presence
Displaying a CONFIDENT PRESENCE that deters predators

Do this by:

- **Keeping your eyes up**

- **Keeping your head up**

- **Walking with erect posture**

- **Using a confident stride**

- **Moving purposefully**

All of these characteristics display a confident presence rather than a weak or easy target presence.

- Do we unconsciously send messages to others that we are afraid and weak?
- Can we change theses unconscious signals we send?

1. **Assertive Presence***: Assertiveness is the ability to exercise one's rights without denying the rights of others. We express our assertiveness with our body language, eye contact and voice. The opposite of assertive is to be inclined to timidity or lack of self-confidence. There are times when an assertive presence is needed in our interpersonal communications.

2. **Defensive Presence***: A defensive presence is only used when dealing with an aggressive individual(s). To avoid being seen as aggressive, stand with your body angled at forty-five degrees to another person. Most animals, when wanting to fight, will signal this approach by facing head on.

The Law of Cause and Effect basically states that for every movement of energy—such as in a natural happening, or a human thought that takes the form of an image, feeling, desire, belief, expectation or action—there is a corresponding effect. For this reason, the Law of Cause and Effect influences every aspect of your living experience. To determine why your living experience is of a certain quality, or why something has come into your life, you simply need to discover what causes preceded the effects. If and when you like the affects you are living with, then you keep the causes. If not, then you change the causes to create a different effect.

How does this help you avoid violence? Using your confident, assertive or defensive presence even when you do not feel like it can influence your thoughts and the situation. The same is true with our thoughts; when we have confident, assertive or defensive thoughts it can influence our bodies and the situation.

Guest/Client Violence

Patient, client or customer violence can involve verbal threats, threatening behavior or physical assaults by an assailant who either receives services from, or is under the custodial supervision of, the affected workplace or the victim.

Violence by clients, patients, guests and customers account for the majority of non-fatal injuries related to workplace violence in many states.

Guest/client violence is often the result of:

- **Intoxication**
- **Mental illness**
- **Anger/aggression**
- **Stress/confusion**
- **Physical abnormalities**
- **Sexual & physical aggression**

Lateral Violence

Lateral violence is often perpetrated by someone who was recently disciplined or discharged. It involves verbal threats, threatening behavior or physical assaults by an assailant who has some employment-related involvement with the workplace. Assailants could be a current or former employee, supervisor, manager, or contractor.

Any workplace can be at risk of violence by a co-worker.

Perpetrated by co-workers, lateral violence includes:

- **Bullying**
- **Intimidation**
- **Anger/aggression**
- **Sexual & physical aggression**
- **May have been recently disciplined or discharged**

> ⇒ **See it**
> ⇒ **Hear it**
> ⇒ **Report it**

Warning Signs of Lateral Violence

Recognizing early warning signs of Lateral Violence

No single sign alone should cause concern, but a combination of any of the following signs should be cause for concern and action:

- Direct or verbal threats of harm.

- Intimidation of others by words and or actions.

- Refusing to follow policies.

- Hypersensitivity or extreme suspiciousness.

- Extreme moral righteousness.

> ⇒ **See it**
> ⇒ **Hear it**
> ⇒ **Report it**

- Inability to take criticism regarding job performance.

- Holding a grudge, especially against a supervisor.

- Repeatedly verbalizing that something will happen to the other person against whom the individual has the grudge.

- Expression of extreme desperation over recent problems.

- Intentional disregard for the safety of others.

- Destruction of property.

An assailant who commits a threat or assault may be seeking revenge for a perceived unfair treatment. Lateral workplace violence fatalities can receive a lot of media attention, but only account for a small portion of all workplace violence related fatalities. Again, stranger violence accounts for most workplace violence fatalities.

Any workplace can be at risk of violence by a co-worker.
An assailant who commits a threat or assault may be seeking revenge for a perceived unfair treatment.

> ⇒ **See it**
> ⇒ **Hear it**
> ⇒ **Report it**

See it, Hear it, Report it

Pre-Incident Reporting: Signs of lateral violence should be reported via your incident reporting procedures.

Domestic Violence

Domestic violence can spill over into the workplace, and often involves:

- **Significant others (spouse, lover, current or not)**
- **Family members (parents, siblings, etc.)**
- **Child custody issues**
- **Stalking**
- **Enemies**
- **Friends**

Domestic violence in the workplace can involve verbal threats, threatening behavior or physical assaults by an assailant who has a personal relationship with someone in the workplace, but does not work in the same workplace. The assailant's actions may be motivated by real or perceived difficulties in the relationship, or psychosocial factors specific to them.

More and more, domestic violence is spilling over into workplace violence. This is a terrifying trend, because you and your employees or co-workers could be in danger from someone you've never met and may not even recognize if he/she came into your workplace.

Women are disproportionately affected by Intimate Partner Violence, Sexual Violence, and stalking.
- Nearly 1 in 5 women (19.3%) and 1 in 59 men (1.7%) have been raped in their lifetime.
- Approximately 1.9 million women were raped during the year preceding the survey.
- One in 4 women (22.3%) have been the victim of severe physical violence by an intimate partner, while 1 in 7 men (14.0%) have experienced the same.
- One in 6 women (15.2%) have been stalked during their lifetime, compared to 1 in 19 men (5.7%).
– **The National Intimate Partner and Sexual Violence Survey (CDC).**

Possible Signs of Victimization
Studies by the ABA **http://www.americanbar.org**, and the FBI **(https://www.fbi.gov/stats-services/publications/workplace-violence)** cite these things as indicators of possible domestic violence or stalking:

The Following Observable Behavior May Suggest Possible Victimization

- Tardiness or unexplained absences
- Frequent-and often unplanned-use of leave time
- Anxiety
- Lack of concentration

- Change in job performance
- Discomfort when communicating with others
- A tendency to remain isolated from coworkers or reluctance to participate in social events
- Disruptive phone calls or e-mail
- Sudden or unexplained requests to be moved from public locations in the workplace, such as sales or reception areas
- Frequent financial problems indicating lack of access to money
- Unexplained bruises or injuries
- Noticeable change in use of makeup (to cover up injuries)
- Inappropriate clothes (e.g., sunglasses worn inside the building, turtleneck worn in the summer)
- Disruptive visits from current or former intimate partner
- Sudden changes of address or reluctance to divulge where she is staying
- Acting uncharacteristically moody, depressed, or distracted
- In the process of ending an intimate relationship; breakup seems to cause the employee undue anxiety
- Court appearances
- Being the victim of vandalism or threats

EAP = Employee Assistance Program

Protecting the Workplace from Domestic Violence

How Do You Protect Yourself From Domestic Violence In The Workplace?

1. Institute a culture of safety in your workplace—that means making people feel SAFE about reporting abuse. Often, a co-worker will report the things listed above. Encourage your employees to go to their supervisors and security personnel if they see anyone has been abused, if they've witnessed stalking behavior, or if they suspect a co-worker has been abused or is being stalked.

2. Remember, the abuse victim IS a victim. Be as subtle and considerate as possible when pulling this person aside to discuss what is going on in her/his home life. Explain to her/him that this DOES affect the workplace, and that, for the safety of this person at work, AND all co-workers, you are obligated to document the abuse. Again, please remember: you are dealing with a victim. Do not victimize her/him again.

3. Get the name, description, and, if at all possible, a photo of the abuser. Many abusers already have a criminal record, and mug shots are in the public domain.

4. Make sure ALL relevant personnel have this photo, and that they know what steps to take. If the victim has filed a restraining order, the front-line personnel need to DISCREETLY call 911.

5. If an employee comes to supervisors to report abuse, TAKE IT SERIOUSLY.

More and more, domestic violence is spilling over into the workplace. Abusive husbands, boyfriends, wives, girlfriends and stalkers are pursuing their victims into their places of work. That puts you at risk. You, everyone who works with you, and your patients, customers and clients.

Extreme Violence

Extreme violence in the workplace/society may include acts of terrorism, active shooters, serial rapists or killers, and sociopaths and psychopaths. Extreme violence goes beyond the human understanding of how and why members of the same species can inflict such pain and harm on one another.

Extreme Violence is often the result of:

- **Terrorism**
- **Active shooters**
- **Sociopaths**
- **Serial rapists**
- **Serial killers**
- **Psychopaths**

Terrorism: the use of violence and intimidation in the pursuit of political aims.

Active Shooters: is an individual(s) actively engaged in killing or attempting to kill people in a confined and populated area. Active Shooter awareness, preparedness and responses will be covered in-depth in Chapter 12.

Serial Rapist: is a person who forces a series of victims into unwanted sexual activity.

Serial Killers: is a person who murders three or more people, usually in service of abnormal psychological gratification.

Sociopaths: a person with a personality disorder manifesting itself in extreme antisocial attitudes and behavior with a lack of conscience.

Psychopaths: a person suffering from chronic mental disorder with abnormal or violent social behavior.

Developing Your Avoidance Ability

Of course, you have a lot more tools for avoidance than just a confident presence. Learning to use all the tools at your disposal will help you develop your avoidance ability.

Structural Avoidance: The use of any barrier, shield, device or protective layer around you. Most commonly these are your home, vehicle, and workplace, and the security that they afford you.

✳ **Behavioral Avoidance:** The ability to recognize behaviors through reading body language is the oldest communication system. Trust in your ability to read others and know that you, too, are sending a message.

Psychological Avoidance: Mental awareness is having the ability to recognize dangers and make decisions, choices and responses that always keep you safe.

Physiological Avoidance: Having the ability to physically and defensively intervene in a situation. Your confident presence is also a huge physiological deterrent.

Environmental Avoidance: Using safety awareness for the different types of environments you are in. Similar to structural avoidance, but more broad in scope as our environments are broad.

Intuitive Avoidance: When you are truly present in the moment, you can receive messages internally and externally. Trusting and acting on the messages will keep you aware and safe.

Chapter 6: Interpersonal Communications

Interpersonal communications is a transactional process through which people share their ideas and feelings by simultaneously sending and receiving messages.

It's a complex and dynamic process in which individuals interact with one another, usually face-to-face. Messages may be exchanged verbally or non-verbally and may be sent intentionally or unintentionally.

> *"The meeting of two personalities is like the contact of two chemical substances: if there is any reaction, both are transformed."*
>
> - Carl Jung, Swiss Psychologist, 1875 – 1961

Interpersonal Communication Skills Involve

Our ability to communicate with others can significantly reduce the potential for conflicts. Interpersonal communications skills involve the following:

* **Active Listening**

* **Asserting**

* **Influencing**

* **Persuading**

* **Empathizing**

* **Sensitivity**

* **Diplomacy**

Active Listening: Active listening is a structured way of listening and responding to others. It focuses attention on the other person. Active listening is, arguably, the most important communication skill of all, because without it, no other technique, theory or principle will work.

- o Webster defines Active as: "involving action or participation"
- o Webster defines Listen (verb) as: "to hear something with thoughtful attention, give consideration"

When we use active listening we are actively involved in hearing and paying attention to what the other person is saying.

When using active listening you should:

- Pay attention to the inflection of the persons words
- Pay attention to the context of what they ae saying
- Use supportive body language – eye communication (shows you are interested)
- Avoid rolling your eyes
- Avoid repeatedly rubbing your neck,
- Avoid looking away often
- Avoid unconsciously shaking your head back and forth (this say's "no")
- Avoid shuffling your feet
- Avoid crossing arms, tapping fingers, biting lip etc.…
- Avoid checking your cell phone, writing notes, texting, etc.…

Asserting: To state or express positively one's rights, beliefs or positions. The caveat to this communication skill is that our rights and beliefs should not affect other people's rights and belief. When we are assertive we state our position in a strong and definite professional way. There are times (not all the time!) in our communication where we must be assertive.

Influencing: Our power to affect people, actions and events. The ability to influence others is more than just using words; it involves our body language and are para-language (tone and inflection).

Persuading: To succeed in causing a person to do, or consent to do, something. We are all in the SALES business. We are either selling an idea, a product or a service. In some cases we are selling all three. Your ability to communicate through persuasion helps you accomplish your goal of serving others, getting your idea across or selling your product. To be persuasive one MUST believe in what one is doing, selling or providing. It's not what you do, it's how you do it that influences and persuades others.

Empathizing: To sense and understand someone else's feelings as if they were one's own. In other words, putting yourself in another person's shoes. This can be difficult at times as some situations are extremely difficult to imagine or entertain being in that person's shoes. However, the key to these situations is to "try" to put yourself in their shoes. When we "try" it comes across in our verbal and non-verbal communication and people recognize our empathy. Empathy is the capacity to understand or feel what another being is experiencing from within the other persons frame of reference. Using empathy fulfills a person's need for psychological survival. We all need to feel understood.

Sensitivity: Being cognizant of emotional feelings (of self and others). A person who is not sensitive in their communication comes across as callous and not caring. Being sensitive when communicating with others demonstrates that you truly care for them. Sensitivity is expressed in our words, tone, inflection and body language.

Diplomacy: Having tact and skill in dealing with people in an effective way. Not having diplomacy in our communications is communicating ineffectually. A person who has tact and skill in their communication will not always say what is on their mind. The opposite of this is a person who does not have a filter and say's whatever is on their mind. Being mindful of what we say is the key to diplomacy. In relationships, business deals, and in situations where we deal with difficult people, diplomacy is absolutely necessary.

Developing Your Communication Skills
(Interpersonal Communication Skills: IPC)

Communication skills involve much more than just speaking well. Albert Mehrabian was a pioneer researcher of body language. In his book, *Nonverbal Communication,* he explained that:

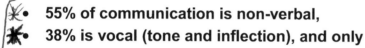

- **55% of communication is non-verbal,**
- **38% is vocal (tone and inflection), and only**
- **7% is verbal (words only).**

Our attitudes and emotions are continuously revealed on our faces—and most of us are completely unaware of it. Most people form 60% to 80% of their initial opinion about a new person in just a few minutes. To communicate effectively, you need to understand the 93% of communication that isn't verbal. Know what message you're sending—and accurately read the message being sent to you.

It's well known that good **communication** is the foundation of any successful relationship, be it personal or professional. It's important to recognize, though, that it's our **nonverbal communication**—our facial expressions, gestures, eye contact, posture, and tone of voice—that speak the loudest.

- Over 90% of our communication is non-verbal.
- Most people are unconscious of their non-verbal communication.
- When reading another person's non-verbal communication look for clusters.
- When individuals are stressed, angered, intoxicated or combative they will focus more on your non-verbal communication and less on your spoken words.
- Failure to pick up on incongruent verbal and non-verbal messages can be tragic.

Facial Expressions
A Smile is worn on every friendly face.
Smiling and laughing are universally considered to be signals that show a person is happy. Smiling serves much the same purpose as it does with other primates: it tells another person you are non-threatening and asks them to accept you on a personal level.

Eye Contact (Limit it to a few seconds 5 sec)

The Three I's Of Eye Communication

• **Intimate** (signals interest in a person)

• **Intimidating** (a person will stare to intimidate or dominate another)

• **Interested** (the category of eye contact recommended for appropriate interpersonal communications).

Give the amount of eye contact that makes others feel comfortable and that you are interested in them. When talking, we maintain 40% to 60% eye contact, with an average of 80% when listening. To build good rapport with people, your eye contact should meet theirs about two-thirds of the time. (The exception to this is Japanese and some Asian and South American cultures where extended eye contact can be seen as aggressive or disrespectful.)

We have all heard that the eyes are the window to the soul. But, what does this really tell us?

Reading Eye Communications:
- **Looking up:** indicates a person is thinking.
- **Looking down:** signal of submission.
- **Looking sideways:** can indicate distraction, showing interest in something, or irritation.
    - ○ **Side-to-Side:** shiftiness, lying or looking for an escape route.
- **Glancing:** may indicate a person wants something.
    - ○ **Target glance:** indicates a person is looking at the striking area.
- **Staring:** may indicate shock, disbelief, aggressiveness or derangement.
- **Tears:** indicates sadness, extreme fear, or tears of joy.
- **Blinking:** blinking a lot can indicate significant stress and non-blinking can indicate attack
- **Pupil Size:** the pupils are affected by light and can also be affected by intoxication.

- **Dilated:** cocaine, crack, meth, hallucinogens and other stimulants
- **Constricted:** heroin, depressants and opioid's

Body Language

- **Body language is an outward reflection of a person's emotional condition.**
- **Positive body language is linked to emotions, so changing your body language can change your attitude.**
- **Postures and Gestures:**
  - **Stand up straight when talking and lean slightly forward when listening.**

When a person has a nervous, negative or defensive attitude it is very likely they will fold their arms firmly on their chest, displaying that they feel threatened. Crossed arms on the chest are universally perceived as defensive or negative.

Gestures: Be expressive, but don't overdo it. Keep your fingers closed when you gesture, hands below chin level and avoid arm or feet crossing. Nodding the head is almost universally used to indicate "yes" or agreement. Using multiple nods can be a persuasion tool. Research shows that people will talk three to four times more than usual when the listener nods their head in regular intervals.

Postures and Gestures

Hands: The hands have been the most important tools in human evolution. There are more connections between the brain and the hands than any other body parts.

Throughout history, the open palm has been associated with truth, honesty, allegiance and submission. Hidden palms may give a person an intuitive feeling that the person they are communicating with is untruthful.

Universal hand signals are:

- **Palms Up = Open**
- **Palms Out = Stop**
- **Palms Down = Authority**
- **Bladed = Defensive**
- **Clenched = Aggressive**

The "Right" Angle

When approaching individuals who are in the assault cycle (stressed, intoxicated, angry, combative), we should approach at a 45-degree angle versus approaching them head on. This type of approach reduces tension and is a safer.

Cultural Differences:

The biggest cultural differences exist mainly in relation to territorial space (distance), eye contact, touching, and insult gestures. The regions that have the greatest number of different gestures are Arab countries and parts of Asia and Japan. Be sensitive to cultural differences if they exist.

_____
_____
_____
_____
_____
_____

Components of the Assault Cycle

The **Assault Cycle** is the predictable behavior that leads to violence. Understanding the Assault Cycle is crucial to knowing how to deescalate and defuse a potentially dangerous situation to break the cycle before violence occurs or escalates.

Use caution when dealing with any of these behaviors, as they can be violence-predicting factors: **stress, intoxication, anger and combative** actions.

   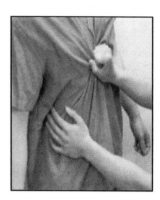

The following information will help you recognize the signs and symptoms of the behaviors as well as give you verbal and physical maneuvers to defuse and avoid violent behaviors.

Stress: Physical, emotional or mental strain or tension brought on by internal and external factors.

Signs and Symptoms of Stress

Aggression & Violence Predicting Factors

• **Change in Facial Expression—flushing**

• **Change in Eye Contact—darting, movement**

• **Change in Speech—speeding up or slowing down**

• **Nervous Nuances—twitching lips/face**

• **Shallow Breathing**

• **Acting Distracted or Confused**

• **Pacing and Fidgeting**

Stress De-Escalation

Use these verbal and physical maneuvers and interventions to defuse and avoid violent behavior:

- **Blade Your Body** so the other person does not feel threatened. (See exercise below)

- **Use You Voice:** slow, quiet and confident tone.

- **Control your Behavior.** If you get agitated, you will escalate the situation. Do not get sucked into the issue. Remember, **I + R = O.**

- **Assess your Body Language**—what signals are you sending? Avoid being rigid. Staying relaxed will encourage the other person to relax.

- **Use Names (individual's and yours)** Introduce yourself and ask the individual their name. Personalizing a situation can reduce tension and establish a bond.

- **Assess Area and Space** you're in, and **stay at least 4' away** and know your escape routes.

- **Do Not Touch the Individual.** Touching a person may escalate the situation.

- **Break Eye Contact** to remain non-threatening and use your interested eye contact.

- **Use Attentive Listening.** Make sure the individual feels like he/she is being listened to.

- **Do NOT make Promises** that you cannot keep.

- **Clarify Communications, and Ask for Specific Responses.**

  - "You want _____, is that correct?" "What can I do to help you?" "I sense you are upset?"

- **Express Your Intention to Help.** "I am here to help." "Is there anything I can get you?"

- **Redirect Environment.** We redirect environments by getting people to move to a new location or area. Moving a person to another location allows them to "save face" (respect) if there are friends and family near. It may also provide you a safer location to deal with them.

- **Redirect Thoughts.** We redirect thoughts by asking questions and questions are powerful. Properly asked questions can enable the person posing them to de-escalate the entire situation.

Learning to Ask the Right Questions

By learning to ask the right questions at the right time, you will be able to:

- Make a positive first impression.
- Positively direct the interaction/situation.
- Control the conversational cadence.
- Stay on task, and not get distracted or sucked into the situation.
- Interrupt the negative momentum.
- Influence another person's behavior as well as your own.
- Direct another person's focus as well as your own.
- Motivate others as well as yourself.
- Develop relationships.
- Establish rapport.
- Set clear goals and make decisions.

When it comes to establishing and understanding effective communications; questions are critical!

Asking a question based on something the other person said demonstrates that you listened.

The Bladed Stance

Dealing with people who are: stressed, angered, intoxicated or physically combative – always BLADE your body.

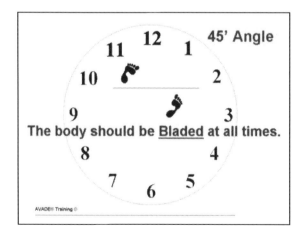
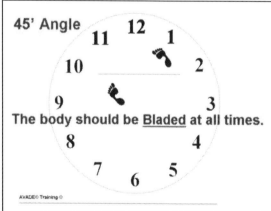

The bladed stance is done by simply turning your body slightly to the side. This stance protects your vulnerable line (nose to groin) as you are now at an angled position. This position is less threatening to others and provides less of a target to an aggressor if the situation escalates. The bladed position can also be done from a seated position.

Anger

Signs and Symptoms of Anger

Anger is a feeling related to one's perception of having been offended or wronged and a tendency to undo that wrongdoing by retaliation. Anger may lead to a person becoming combative if the person is unable to maintain control. All of us have been angry, and how we handle our anger and deal with another person's anger can determine the kind of outcome we want.

Signs and Symptoms of Anger (Aggression & Violence Predicting Factors)

- **Loud Voice**

- **Challenging Statements**

- **Foul Language**

- **Verbal Threats**
    - ○ **Veiled Threats**
    - ○ **"What do you mean by_____"**
- **Physically Acting Out (Pacing & Tense)**

- **Personal History of Violence**
  (Knowledge of a person's background and history can be extremely important as it can be a pre-incident indicator of escalation to violence).

- **Exaggerated Movements**

- **Demanding Expressions**

- **Demanding**
    - ○ **unnecessary services**
    - ○ **unnecessary attention**
    - ○ **entitlement**
- **Acting Disgruntled**

- **Attempting to Intimidate (by invading a person's personal space)**

Anger De-Escalation

Remember to use all interventions for stressed individuals, and *use these* verbal and physical maneuvers to defuse and avoid violent behavior.

Above all, control your own emotions and remember this **QTIP:**

- **Quit Taking It Personally.** When your buttons get pushed, because you are being yelled at, cursed at, intimidated etc., you end up taking things personally. This never helps! Remember to quit taking things personally, be professional and be nice.

- **Walk Away if Possible.** Yes, just walk away.

- **Avoid Arguing.** No one ever really wins an argument. So avoid arguing and telling someone they are wrong. Instead use this powerful phrase: *"If I were in your shoes, I would probably feel the same way."*

- **Don't Interrupt—allow them to vent.** Interrupting a person is the quickest and surest way to tell them that you are not listening and that your thoughts and ideas are more important than theirs.

- **Display Sincerity.** Sincerity means freedom from deceit, hypocrisy, or duplicity. The ancient word "sincere" means without wax. When we are sincere, we are real.
    - People know when individuals are being fake. Be sincere!

- **Seek to Agree—and get them to say "yes."** When we agree another person or get them to agree with us, it builds a bond.
    Example: "You're right, this place does stink." "Yeah, it is overcrowded in here, huh."

- **Use a Collaborative Approach—using "we" and "us"—gives a person a feeling of belonging. Example:** "Why don't we sit down and talk about this." "Between us we will come up with something." "Why don't we go outside and talk about this."

- **Identify the Problem. Ask them "I sense you are angry/upset?"** Using this technique gets to the issue, versus dancing around the issue. There may be a simple solution or fix it for the person who is angry.

- People who are asked this question ("I sense you are angry/upset") will generally tell you why they are angry/upset. With the information received, you may be able to offer a resolution to the problem.

- **Give Options. Expressing feelings like the angry person has a choice may help them choose to calm down.** People don't like absolutes, they like options. Always offer the best option first and less desirable options after. It puts the "ball in their court" so to speak.

- **Resist Being Defensive.**

  - **do not make threats**
  - **ignore challenges**

When we are defensive or make threats and challenges, we become the aggressive individual. Remember QTIP and don't go down in the mud with the individual. If you feel like you are getting sucked into the situation, remove yourself. The old saying "good cop, bad cop" needs to be replaced with "good cop, better cop.. Let someone else take over where you left off.

- **Set and Enforce Boundaries, but only ones you can enforce.** Initially, we allow people to vent. But, when people vent and continue to vent, you may need to intervene and set boundaries. If you say you are going to do something, you need to be able to back it up. In parenting, we call this tough love.

- **Ask Questions rather than Give Orders!** What are the common problems that you face in your workplace on a frequent basis? Identify what they are and instead of ordering a person to not do what they are doing. Replace it with a question.

Example: Order: "Sir, you can't smoke here."

Question: "Sir, did you know this is a non-smoking area?"

Example: Order: "Miss, you can't park your car here."

Question: "Miss, did you know this is valet parking only?"

Asking a question versus giving and order gives a person an out. It allows them to save face, develops a rapport with them and provides the compliance that you are looking for.

Intoxication

Intoxication (also known as drunkenness, inebriation, being high, under-the-influence, etc.) is a physiological state occurring when an individual has a high level of alcohol or drugs in their bloodstream. Intoxication can lower inhibitions and impair self-control, leading to violence. Anyone under the influence of alcohol or drugs—prescription or otherwise—falls into this category.

Signs and Symptoms of Intoxication

Signs of Intoxication Include:
(Aggression & Violence Predicting Factors)

- **Slurred Speech**

- **Impaired balance and/or poor coordination**

- **Flushed face**

- **Frequent rubbing of nose, or twisting jaw back and forth**

- **Abnormal eyes- red, glossy, pupils dilated**

- **Up & Down Attitudes—euphoria, despair, etc.**

- **Reduced inhibition, erratic behavior**

- **Acting paranoid or disconnected**

- **Odors, on breath and/or clothing**

- **Emotional Response**

- **Argumentative**

- **Loud and Obnoxious**

Intoxication De-Escalation

Remember to use stress and anger intervention techniques, as well as the verbal and physical maneuvers listed below, to defuse and avoid violent behavior with intoxicated individuals.

- **Avoid** intoxicated individuals **when at all possible.** The best de-escalation for intoxicated individuals is avoidance.

- **Use Caution and Stay Aware.** When you can't avoid intoxicated individuals be sure to stay aware and use caution. When people are intoxicated they are impaired. When impaired, people will do things they wouldn't normally do when they are sober.

- **Don't Argue. Arguing** with intoxicated individuals **can escalate** the situation. Arguing never helps the situation, especially with a person who is under the influence, therefor, not necessarily rationale.

- **Be Proactive in your Responses.** Reactive responses are always delayed. Proactive people recognize that proactive responses are preferred.

- **Seek to Agree.** The intoxicated individual usually wants an ally. When we seek to agree with them it builds that ally, which ultimately builds a rapport with them. Having a rapport equals less chance of escalation.

- **Express your Feelings**—expressing that you are frightened or scared of the person's behavior may de-escalate them.
  Example: "That really scared me when you said that."
  Example: "I am concerned, as I care about you and your safety."

- **Assess Area and Space—for weapons, escape routes and maintain a proper distance from them.** In Chapter 9 we discuss weapons and the appropriate distance to be from them. With an intoxicated individual a weapon may be anything. Be aware of what is around you and within reach of the intoxicated person. Know your escape routes and remember you need to be at least 4' away from an individual to avoid an unarmed attack.

Above all else, maintain your awareness!

Combative Aggression

Signs and Symptoms of Combative Physical Aggression
(Aggression & Violence Predicting Factors)

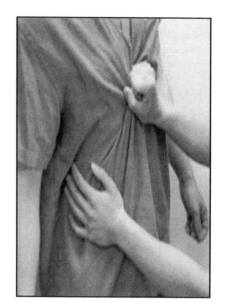

- **Changes in Posture—dropping into a fighting stance (pugilistic stance)**

- **Preparatory Signals—rolls sleeves up, takes coat off, etc. or stands up suddenly**

- **Scanning Area by Moving Head Side to Side**

- **Non or Slow Blinking Pattern ("thousand-yard stare")**

- **Flanking Positioning (finding a suitable position to attack)**

- **Telegraphing Intentions—arm swings or gets cocked before a punch is thrown**

- **Looks at Striking Area—an assailant will almost always look at the area they intend to strike before the attack (target glance)**

- **Exaggerated Movements (lunging in)**

- **Changes in Verbalization—either talking a lot more, or suddenly talking less**
- **Bracing Effect—as though bracing to hit or be hit**

- **Tightening of Body and/or Fists (clenching)**

- **Trying to Distract YOU**

A combative individual(s) is in constant state of communication. Therefore, their intent, thought processes, cues, signs, and signals are always leaking out—through the body, paralanguage, and the actual words used.

It is critical that YOU learn these danger signals!

Strategies to Avoid Physical Harm with a Combative Person Defined

- **Escape Immediately.** That is the most important thing you can do. Once someone has reached the state of combative aggression, your number one priority is to get away. The best self-defense is to not be there! Escape-Escape-Escape.

- **Defensive Presence.** Show that you're ready to defend yourself by blading your body and hands. A defensive presence demonstrates that you are trained and ready to defend yourself if needed. A defensive presence should only be used in a combative situation, otherwise it could escalate a situation be sending a message that you are aggressive.

- **Loud Scream or Yell** so you can attract attention. Yelling, "Stop!" can also arrest someone's attack. Yelling or screaming loudly will alert others, create witnesses, establish your authority, keep you breathing, can be used to distract, provides direction to the aggressor, and reduces liability risk to you and your agency.

- **Use Distractions** to interrupt their focus and intent. Distractions buy us time to escape, defend or control. Distractions interrupt one or more of the five senses, giving you time to act. Distractions are: sounds, movements, psychological and lights. Always use Distractions!

- **Stay Aware and Avoid Tunnel Vision.** When your heart rate exceeds 145 beats per minute your vision narrows causing what is called "tunnel vision." Knowing this, you can be aware and avoid it by physically turning your head side to side.

- **Watch to see what they are planning to do next.** Awareness is always the key component in dealing with combative individuals. Anticipating what the combatant will do next gives us time and time is precious.

- **Get Help: Alert Others** by motioning or verbalizing. There is safety in numbers! Many agencies have "emergency codes" for combative persons. Know your codes, and how to initiate them.

- **Last Resort: Defend or Control if escape is impossible!** If you cannot get away, you are left with only two options (being a victim is not an option), defend yourself, and/or control the out of control individual.

Submission
To yield or surrender (oneself) to the will or authority of another.

Just as important as knowing the signal of escalation is knowing the signals of submission. Submission is displayed through a significant cluster of body movements that are used to signal fear and readiness to submit. This is common in humans and animals, where fighting (that could terminally harm each animal) is avoided by displays of aggression or submission.

Signs & Symptoms of Submission

- **Body Positions:** In fearful stances the body is generally closed and may also include additional aspects.

- **Self-Protection:** Hunching inwards reduces the size of the body, limiting the potential of being hit and protecting vital areas; for example, hands covering crotch or chin pushed down to protect the neck.

  - In a natural setting, being small may also reduce the chance of being seen. Arms are held in. A crouching position may be taken, even slightly with knees slightly bent. This is approaching the curled-up, regressive fetal position.

- **Lowering:** Putting the body in a lower position shows the other person that you are not a physical threat. This can include hunching down, bowing, kneeling or even prostration. It is no surprise that these are typically used in formal greetings of a superior person. Even in sitting, a submissive person will choose a lower chair or slump in order to be lower than others are.

- **Motionlessness:** By staying still, the chance of being seen is, in a natural setting, reduced (which is why many animals freeze when they are fearful). When exposed, it also reduces the chance of accidentally sending signals which may be interpreted as being aggressive. It also signals submission, in that you are ready to be struck and will not fight back.

- **Head Down:** Turning the chin and head down protects the vulnerable neck from attack. It also avoids looking the other person in the face (staring is a sign of aggression).

- **Eyes Down:** Widening the eyes makes you look more like a baby and hence signals your vulnerability. Looking attentively at the other person shows that you are hanging on to their every word.

- **Mouth (Smile):** Submissive people smile more at dominant people, but they often smile with the mouth but not with the eyes.

- **Submissive Gestures:** There are many gestures that have the primary intent of showing submission and that there is no intent to harm the other person. Hands out and palms up shows that no weapons are held and is a common pleading gesture. Other gestures and actions that indicate tension may indicate the state of fear. This includes hair tugging, face touching and jerky movement. There may also be signs such as whiteness of the face and sweating.

- **Small Gestures:** When the submissive person must move, then small gestures are often made. These may be slow to avoid alarming the other person, although tension may make them jerky.

- **Submissive Verbalization:** Common verbalization will be; "I'm sorry," "I shouldn't have…," "I didn't mean to," "I apologize," "What can I do?" "You're right; I'm wrong," etc.

- **Wanting to Shake Your Hand:** An individual may want to shake your hand as an expression of their submission. Caution! When shaking a person's hand we are within the reactionary gap (4' zone) and may be vulnerable to an attack. This tactic could be a ploy to lead you into the attack zone.

> **Dealing with people who are stressed, angry, intoxicated or combative can be a frightening experience. For some it is part of their daily experience at their workplace. No matter what you do, your interpersonal communications can help you recognize and diffuse a potentially violent situation.**

Developing and Using Your IPC (Interpersonal Communication Skills)

Some general things to keep in mind when communicating:

- **Be Clear and Concise when Speaking**

- **Avoid using Slang and Jargon** when speaking to people. It helps avoid confusion, misdirection, complaints and poor interpersonal relations.

- **Play the Part of the Scene you are in...**"All the world is indeed a stage and we are merely players." As the stage changes, play the appropriate part to keep yourself and others safe.

- **The Golden Rule (treating others as you would like to be treated)** Treating and speaking to people with respect is a universally accepted standard of treating people. "Do unto others as you would have them do unto you."

- **Platinum Rule**
  (treat others the way *they* want to be treated)

- **Use Common Courtesies** consistently and repeatedly with all people, all the time.
  - Please.
  - Thank you.
  - Yes, please.
  - My pleasure.
  - You're welcome.
  - I am sorry to disturb you, but I need to speak with you a moment.

- **People Watch and Pay Attention.** Watch and learn as you view the stage that others are on. Pay attention to what works and doesn't work for you and other people.

- **Learn from your experiences and the experiences of others.**

Experience is a great teacher!
Knowledge, training and experiences are the keys to understanding and avoiding situations that are threatening and unsafe. When faced with a situation that is unavoidable and threatening, we may need to physically intervene to defend ourselves or another person.

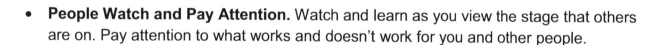
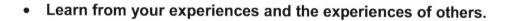

Chapter 7: Defense of Self and Others

> *"The best and safest thing is to keep a balance in your life, acknowledge the great powers around us and in us. If you can do that, and live that way, you are really a wise man."* – Euripides, Greek dramatist (484-406 B.C.)

What is Self-Defence?

Self-defense is the right to use *reasonable* force to protect one's self or members of one's staff/family from bodily harm from the attack of an aggressor if you have reason to believe that you or they are in danger. Self-defense must always be your last resort. When it is used, the force used must be considered "reasonable"; i.e., striking someone who yells an obscenity at you is not considered "reasonable force."

The best self-defense is to avoid the situation and get away. If avoidance and escape are not possible, a reasonable defense would be lawful as a last resort. You have the right to defend yourself; however, any use of self-defense must follow any agency policy and procedure, as well as follow state and federal law.

The following information will provide a general understanding of what self-defense and use of force are, and how you can legally protect yourself against assault and liability risk associated with any type of self-defense or force.

Disclaimer

This chapter will give you a basic understanding of self-defense, assault, reasonable force and basic legal definitions of force. Personal Safety Training Inc. makes no legal declaration, representation or claim as to what force should be used or not used during a self-defense or assault incident or situation. Each individual must take into consideration their ability, agency policies and procedures, and laws in the state and country in which they reside.

Types of Assault

Physical Assault: The attempt to cause injury, coupled with the present ability to cause injury.

Non-Physical Assault: Physical contact is not required to constitute an assault. In all states, threats are a separate crime. A verbal threat of physical harm is one with the intent to intimidate or scare, with the result altering any part of a person's normal life due to the threat.

To constitute an illegal threat, the following must be true:
- The threat must be serious, with the threat of definite injury
- The threat must be immediate, and can be carried out in the immediate or near future.
- The threat must be credible; that is, the victim believes the threat and acts upon that belief.

Domestic Assault: Can involve battery that occurs between two parties who are related by some degree (family or intimate relationships).

Battery Assault: Battery is a criminal offense whereby one party makes physical contact with another party with the intention to harm them. In order to constitute battery, an offense must be intentional and must be committed to inflict injury on another.

Sexual Battery: Any non-consensual physical contact that is sexual in nature.

Lawful Use of Defense

In order to be lawful in your defense of yourself and others, you must have a basic understanding of some legal definitions and how they apply to self-defense and our legal system.

1. **Use-of-Force**
2. **Reasonable Force**
3. **Reasonable Belief**
4. **Deadly Force**
5. **Excessive Force**
6. **Dangerous & Deadly Weapons**

Use-of-Force

A term that describes the right of an individual or authority to settle conflicts or prevent certain actions by applying measures to either:

- **Dissuade another party from a particular course of action…or**

- **Physically intervene to stop or control them.**

Reasonable Force: The degree of force which is not excessive and is appropriate in protecting one's self or one's property.

- **When such force is used, a person is justified and is not criminally liable, nor is he liable in tort.** (A tort is an act that damages someone in some way, and for which the injured person may sue the wrongdoer for damages.)

Reasonable Belief: The facts or circumstances that an individual knows, or should know, are such as to cause an ordinary and prudent person to act or think in a similar way under similar circumstances.

Deadly Force: Force that is likely or intended to cause death or great bodily harm. Deadly force may be reasonable or unreasonable, depending on the circumstances.

Excessive Force: That amount of force which is beyond the need and circumstances of the particular event, or which is not justified in the light of all the circumstances; as in the case of deadly force to protect property as contrasted with protecting life.

Dangerous and Deadly Weapons

"Dangerous Weapon" is a device or instrument which, in the manner it is used, or intended to be used, is calculated or likely to produce death or great bodily harm.

"Deadly Weapons" includes any firearm, whether loaded or unloaded, or device designed as a weapon and capable of producing death or great bodily harm.

Levels of Force and Defense

The following chart is designed to give you a basic understanding of how your actions may apply to the actions of an aggressive subject. Your action may need to increase or decrease, dependent upon the situation. Any Use-of-Force or Self-Defense MUST be lawful.

Lawful Use-of-Force & Defense is permissible:

1. When used to control an out of control individual

2. When used to overcome resistance of the out of control individual

3. When used to prevent escape from an individual who is under your control (hold)

4. When used in self-defense or in the defense of others

Use-of-Force & Self-Defense MUST be Reasonable

YOU should always take into consideration the facts and the circumstances of the incident.

➡ Type of crime and severity of the crime

➡ Resistance of the subject when needing to control them

➡ The threat and safety to others in the area

➡ Aggressive Subject and Staff Factors

Aggressive Subject and Staff Factors

Many factors may affect your selection of an appropriate level of use-of-force or self-defense. These factors should be articulated in your post incident documentation.

Examples may include:

Age: In dealing with an aggressive subject who is agile, younger, faster, stronger, and has more stamina an older staff person may have to use more force/control/defense. In contrast a younger staff person would use less control/force/defense on an older person.

Size: In dealing with a larger aggressive subject, a smaller staff person may need to use more force/control/defense during the incident. A larger staff person would obviously, use less force/control/defense an aggressive subject who is smaller.

Skill Level: In dealing with a subject who is skilled in mixed martial arts or an expert in karate, it may be more difficult to control or defend against them based on their skill level. A staff person who is skilled in defensive tactics, may only need to use a minimum of force (with proper technique) to control/defend the subject. A staff person without current training and experience may need to use more force/defense to control or defend against the subject.

Relative Strength: The different body composition of males and females may be a factor in controlling a member of the opposite gender. Females typically have less torso strength than their male counterparts. A male staff may have to use less force to control a female subject. Whereas, a female staff person may need to use more force to control a male subject.

Multiple Aggressors: A staff person who is being physically attacked by multiple aggressors is at a disadvantage. Even a highly skilled staff involved in defensive tactics is likely to be harmed in a situation such as this. In order to survive multiple aggressor attacks, higher levels of force may be necessary.

> *Special Note:*
>
> *Every person must take into consideration their moral, legal, and ethical beliefs and rights and understandings when using any type of force to defend themselves or others. Personal Safety Training Inc. makes no legal declaration, representation or claim as to what force should be used or not used during a self-defense/assault incident or situation. Each individual must take into consideration their ability, agency policies and procedures and laws in their state and/or country.*

Post Incident Response

It's vital for all employers to have a Post Incident Response protocol. The following points are guideline for the proper and most efficient response to a violent incident.

Triage (Medical/Hazmat): Triage is the process of determining the priority of patients/victims treatments based on the severity of their condition. Initial first-aid treatment and protocols for hazardous materials/clean-up should be handled immediately.

Report to the Police, Security, Risk Management, Human Resources etc... Follow standard operating procedures in regard to reporting incidents.

Consider All Involved—staff, guests, visitors, patients or anyone who was witness to the incident should be treated accordingly for medical and stress debriefing.

Provide for Incident Debriefing: Debriefing allows those involved with the incident to process the event and reflect on its impact. Depending on the situation, a thorough debriefing may need to take place. Even those not specifically involved in an incident may suffer emotional and psychological trauma.

Critical Incident Stress Debriefing (CISD) is a specific technique designed to assist others in dealing with physical or psychological symptoms that are generally associated with critical incident trauma exposure. Research on the effectiveness of critical incident debriefing techniques has demonstrated that individuals who are provided critical stress debriefing within a 24- to 72-hour window after the critical incident and experience have less short-term and long-term crisis reactions and psychological trauma.

Employee Assistance Programs (EAP) EAPs are intended to help employees deal with work/personal problems that might adversely impact their work performance, health, and well-being. EAPs generally include assessment, short-term counseling and referral services for employees and their household members. Employee benefit programs offered by many employers, typically in conjunction with a health insurance plans, provide for payment for EAPs.

Document incident to include any follow-up investigations: Post incident documentation is absolutely critical for reducing liability risk, preventing reoccurrences and follow-up investigations.

Initiate corrective actions to prevent reoccurrences: Preventing similar future incidents, involves taking proactive corrective actions. Agency management, supervision, security, risk management, employee safety committees, environment of care committees, etc. should initiate, track and follow up on corrective actions

✳ Post Incident Documentation

- **Who-What-Where-When-Why-How**
  The first rule in post incident documentation is the "who, what, where, when, why and how" rule of reporting. After writing an incident narrative, double-check to see if you have included the first rule of reporting.

- **Witnesses (who was there?)**
  Make sure to include anyone who was a witness to the incident. Staff, visitors, guests and support services (police, fire, EMS, etc.) can be valuable witnesses should an incident be litigated.

- **Narrative Characteristics**
  A proper narrative should describe in details the characteristics of the violent offender/predator.

- **Before, During and After**
  A thorough incident report will describe what happened before, during and after the incident. Details matter!

- **1st Person vs. 3rd Person**
  The account of an incident can be described in first person or third person. This can be specific to your agency protocols or the preference of the person documenting the incident.

- **Post Follow-Up (track and trend)**
  Most agencies use electronic documentation, which allows for easy retrieval, tracking and trending. Using technology assists agencies to follow up and initiate proactive corrections.

- **Follow Standard Operating Procedures**
  Whether it is handwriting incident reports or electronic documentation and charting, staff should consistently and thoroughly document all incidents relating to violence in the workplace.

Chapter 8: Stress Management

Stress is physical, emotional or mental strain or tension brought on by internal and external factors.

"If you are distressed by anything external, the pain is not due to the thing itself, but to your estimate of it; and this you have the power to revoke at any moment."

– Marcus Aurelius Antoninus (121 AD - 180 AD)

In 1975, Hans Selye, a doctor of medicine and chemistry, published a model that divides stress into distress and eustress. Persistent stress that is not resolved by a coping mechanism or adaptation is deemed distress. Distress may lead to anxiety, withdrawal, and depression. Stress that enhances functions (physical or mental, such as through strength training or challenging work) is considered eustress.

Types of Stress:

1. **Distress**
2. **Eustress**

The difference between eustress and distress is the result of the stress determined by a person's experience (real or imagined), their expectations, and their resources to cope with the stress.

"Adopting the right attitude can convert a negative stress into a positive one."

– Dr. Hans Selye

FEAR

Fear is a distressing emotion aroused by a perceived threat. It is a basic survival mechanism that occurs in response to a specific stimulus, such as pain or the threat of danger. Some psychologists suggest that fear belongs to a small set of basic or innate emotions. This set also includes such emotions as joy, sadness, and anger. Fear should be distinguished from the related emotional state of anxiety, which typically occurs without any external threat.

Fear may be induced whether the threat is real or imagined.

Additionally, fear is related to the specific behaviors of escape and avoidance, whereas stress is the result of threats that are perceived to be uncontrollable or unavoidable. Worth noting is that fear almost always relates to future events, such as worsening of a situation, or continuation of a situation that is unacceptable. Fear could also be an instant reaction to something presently happening.

"Fight-Flight-Freeze"

You've heard of fight-or-flight, which is a reaction to a threat with a general discharge of the sympathetic nervous system, priming the organism for fighting or fleeing. If completely overwhelmed, a person may freeze.

The **fight-flight-freeze response** is a basic, primal, physiological urge to defend or to flee in times of danger. When faced with a situation that is frightening, your perception of it stimulates the part of the brain called the hypothalamus. The hypothalamus emits a hormone that stimulates the pituitary gland to release substances that excite the adrenal gland to release adrenalin (epinephrine) and cortisone.

- Adrenalin stimulates the heart to beat faster and the vessels carrying blood to the muscles to open.
- The vessels that run the digestive and eliminative organs constrict. Blood pressure goes up, and more blood is being pumped, but many vessels constrict to slow the blood flow.
- Breath becomes faster and shallower, or you hold your breath.
- Blood shunts systematically from the vegetative organs to the muscles preparing you to fight or take flight.

Strategies for Managing your Stress

Putting the Brakes on the Fight-Flight-Freeze

Conscious Controlled Breathing and Conscious Positive Thinking are considered the best stress management techniques for immediate stressors (fight-flight) and ongoing stressors of life.

Conscious Controlled Breathing is a very useful tactic in lowering our blood pressure. Studies have shown that during the process of slow, deep breathing, endorphins are released, causing a feeling of general well-being and relaxation. Endorphins apply a brake to the hypothalamic fight-flight response in a situation of imminent danger. Try this: inhale slowly, about two-thirds of your lung capacity. Breathe in for a count of four seconds; breathe out slowly to a count of eight seconds. Notice you immediately feel calmer.

Conscious Positive Thinking and calm mental preparation were recognized to be highly valuable to the Samurai of feudal Japan. In fact, the Samurai spent as much time in mental training as they did preparing their bodies for battle. Samurai employed two techniques to prepare the mind to be tranquil, fearless, and energetic in combat: breath control and meditation. The Samurai knew that a warrior filled with fear (negative thoughts) is

doomed. Fear inhibits the ability to think quickly or to act fully.

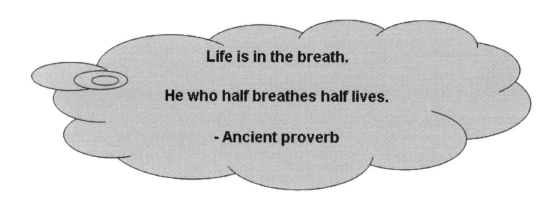

Life is in the breath.

He who half breathes half lives.

- Ancient proverb

Caution!: All strategies and methods for managing your stress should take into consideration your physical and mental health.
Consult your physician prior to any changes in your behavior.

Strategies for Managing Your Stress Before an Incident of Workplace Violence

1. Healthy Eating: Proper nutrition and healthy eating habits can help you get through stressful times. Eating well will increase your physical, mental, and emotional stamina. Fueling yourself with food high in nutrients can boost your immune system, help you maintain a healthy weight and help you feel better about yourself.

2. Regular Exercise: Frequent exercise is one of the best physical stress-reduction techniques. Exercise not only improves your health and reduces stress; it also relaxes tense muscles and helps you to sleep better. Most importantly, there is evidence that suggests that physically fit people have less severe physiological responses when under stress than those who are not.

3. Proper Hydration: Stress can lead to dehydration. Dehydration affects thinking, causes headaches, nausea, constipation and irritability. Water is essential to your wellbeing.

4. Time Management: Planning your day can help you accomplish more and feel more in control of your life. Write a to-do list, putting the most important tasks at the top. Keep a schedule of your daily activities to minimize conflicts and last-minute rushes. Prioritize your tasks and say "no" to nonessential tasks.

5. Positive Thoughts: Negative thoughts and energy can affect you in many ways and cause you additional stress. Because of this, developing more positive thoughts is an important way to reduce stress in your life. You can help yourself maintain and increase positive thoughts by listening to uplifting music, reading inspirational books, spending time with positive people, and using positive affirmations.

6. Touch Therapy: Touch is the first sense to develop in humans. It is essential to our health and wellbeing. Babies have been known to fail to thrive and even die without an adequate amount of physical contact. Adults, as well, can become depressed and ill if they are isolated from this most basic of human needs.

7. Support System: It doesn't take a scientific study to show that surrounding yourself with supportive family, friends and co-workers can have a positive effect on your mental well-being. A strong social support network can be critical to help you through the stress of tough times, whether you've had a bad day at work, or a year filled with loss or chronic illness.

8. Recreation: Recreational activities are experiences in which you actively participate in an organized activity, generally with others, to have fun and enjoy life. They include participation in sports, arts and crafts, games, dancing, or any activity that takes involvement and participation.

9. Nature: Use nature to reduce stress. Go outside, hike in the woods, walk on the beach, anything that puts you in contact with the natural world. It is difficult to feel stressed when you are surrounded by nature's abundance of vitality and wonder.

10. Sacred Space: Sacred space is defined as any place where you're temporarily sealed off from the world. This can be a room, a special chair, even an activity, or just a state of mind. But the idea is that when you're in sacred space, whatever you're doing becomes a meditation or a peaceful state for your mind and body. Creating and maintaining your sacred space is a great way to reduce stress.

Post Incident Stress Debriefing

The methods described above help manage your stress before an incident occurs. The methods described below will help you manage stress after an incident of workplace violence.

- **Always Debrief.** Staff should debrief after every workplace violence incident, regardless of the severity. Oftentimes a brief discussion of the events and outcome is enough. Other times, a more intensive debriefing is needed.
    - o **The goal of debriefing is to reduce the chances of Post-Traumatic Stress Disorder, or PTSD.**

- **Acknowledge Humanness.** As humans we are susceptible to the frailties of human nature. This acknowledgement creates an awareness that it is okay to seek and ask for help.

- **Talk to co-workers.** Almost all workers have experienced or witnessed some type of workplace violence incident. Your co-workers can be a great source to vent your concerns about your post feelings.

- **Be aware of post-event feelings.** Having the knowledge and awareness that you may experience strong feelings from an event can give you the confidence to seek help and discuss feelings with others.

- **Take advantage of your Employee Assistance Program (EAP).** Agencies realize that post feelings may remain for longer periods of time after an incident. Employee Assistance Programs can benefit employees and help them deal with post incident stress or other work/personal problems. EAPs are intended to help employees deal with issues/problems that might adversely affect their work performance, health, and well-being. EAPs generally include assessment, short-term counseling and referral services for employees and their household members.

- **Know the signs and symptoms of Post-Traumatic Stress Disorder (PTSD).** A psychological reaction occurring after experiencing a highly stressing event (such as wartime combat, physical violence, or a natural disaster). PTSD is usually characterized by depression, anxiety, flashbacks, recurrent nightmares, and avoidance of reminders of the event.

- **Take the time to follow-up with other staff.** As human beings, we often focus on the needs of others and not ourselves. Take the time to discuss workplace incidents, your feelings about the incidents, and how incidents in the workplace could improve.

Critical Incident Stress Debriefing (CISD)

- **Debriefing is a specific technique designed to assist people in dealing with the physical or psychological symptoms that are generally associated with trauma exposure.**

- **Debriefing allows those involved with the incident to process the event and reflect on its impact.**

Individuals who are exposed to an assault situation (as a witness or a victim) should consider some level of critical incident debriefing or counseling.

The final extent of any traumatic situation may never be known or realistically estimated in terms of trauma, loss and grief. In the aftermath of any critical incident, psychological reactions are quite common and are fairly predictable. CISD can be a valuable tool following a traumatic event.

Research on the effectiveness of critical incident debriefing techniques has demonstrated that individuals who are provided CISD within a 24- to 72-hour period after the critical incident experience less short-term and long-term crisis reactions, psychological trauma, and PTSD.

Chapter 9: Time and Distance

The concept of time or distance illustrates that having time or distance can give us distance or time from a violent person, place, event or thing. What we do with our time can be the most precious investment we ever make. Imagine that you have the ability to use time and distance to your advantage. And remember:

Time and Distance = Safety

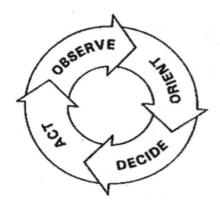

Reaction Time (OODA Loop)

Air Force Colonel John Boyd coined the term "OODA Loop" to describe a form of reaction time and decision-making. OODA stands for: **O**bserve-**O**rient-**D**ecide-**A**ct.

Boyd's key concept is that the decision cycle is the process by which an individual reacts to an event. Accordingly, the key to victory is to be able to create situations wherein one can make appropriate decisions more quickly than one's opponent. This was originally a theory of achieving success in air-to-air combat.

Time is the dominant parameter in the OODA Loop. The individual who goes through the OODA Loop in the shortest time prevails, because his opponent is caught responding to situations that have already changed.

Observation: The collection of relevant data through your senses.
Orientation: The analysis of observed data to form your current mental perspective of what is happening.
Decision: Determining a course of action based on one's current mental perspective.
Action: The physical acting-out of your decisions.

Weapons and Time/Distance

Being faced with a weapon is terrifying. Know what to do ahead of time, and use the OODA Loop to your advantage.

Unarmed Attacks = 4-6' (minimum) You need a distance of at least four to six feet, which will give you time to escape from an attack. Variables that can affect this are environment, distractions and your physical ability.

Clubs and Sticks When encountering an individual with a club, stick, or any type of impact weapon, the best defense is to create the biggest distance between you and them as you can. Studies have shown that individuals with weapons can cover a distance of twenty-one feet in approximately 1.5 seconds.

Knives/Edged or Sharpened Weapons Twenty-one feet is the minimum distance you need from a person with any type of edged weapon. Your use of defense will need to escalate to defend yourself against any type of weapon being used against you. Again, your best defense is always to escape when possible.

Thrown Objects Like the above weapons, a thrown object (chair, table, computer, etc.) can seriously injure an individual. Creating as much distance as possible between you and the aggressor is recommended.

Guns In an active shooter situation, the best defense is to escape or seek cover.
Examples of cover: locations such as a safe room, behind a large barrier that is impenetrable, away from the area in stairwells, elevators, etc.

- Without the ability to seek cover immediately, your best defense is to **RUN!**

- Run, zig-zag, jump and keep moving away until you are in a covered position.

- It is very difficult for a person to hit a moving target.

- Most experienced law enforcement officers/trainers will tell you that a moving target is far harder to hit that a fixed target. Couple that with creating distance and you have a better chance at surviving.

- Active Shooter awareness, preparedness and responses will be covered in-depth in Chapter 12.

- "Gun Threat Response Defense" is covered in AVADE® Level II Self-Defense Tactics and Techniques.

Dangerous Weapons in YOUR workplace

Learn the best way to protect from, and respond to, any use of a regular item that suddenly becomes a weapon.

➡ Pens

Carry your pens so that they cannot be grabbed off of your person and used against you. A pen can easily impale the human body. Pens are a common tool that we all use. Increase your awareness by knowing that they can also harm you when in the hands of an out-of-control, combative individual.

➡ Chairs

Escape immediately if a person has grabbed a chair and is preparing to throw it at you.

➡ Glass/Beverages

Glass and other hard items that hold beverages and food can be thrown or used to strike at you. The contents in these can also be used to assault you—hot beverages such as coffee/tea.

➡ Name Badges/Lanyards - Stethoscopes

Use caution with anything that is around your neck.

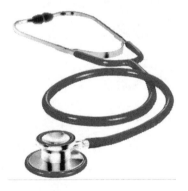

➡ Items that can be moved or picked up.

Anything that can be picked up can be used as a weapon—staplers, heavy binders, small copiers, etc.

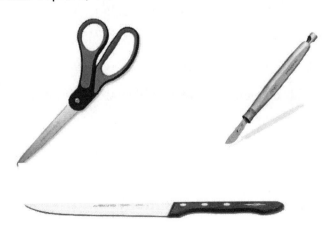

➡ Edged Weapons: scissors, utensils, etc.

Be cautious and aware that edged weapons are almost everywhere in the workplace environment. Kitchen utensils and office items are in most work environments and may pose a threat in the hands of an aggressor.

The Art of Distraction

The Art of Distraction **is a process by which you can buy valuable time to Escape, Control or Defend.** Distractions affect the senses, which take time for the mind to process the new information. They mainly affect a person's sight and sense of hearing; however, psychological distractions, such as asking a person something completely out of the ordinary can cause a mental delay as well. Distractions have been used since ancient times and are a valuable advantage you should always use.

➡ **Sounds:** Using a loud scream or yell can cause a momentary delay.
➡ **Movements:** Using your hands, eyes, and body can distract and cause a momentary delay.
➡ **Psychological:** Asking a person something completely out of the ordinary can cause them to have a mental delay. (i.e., "What color socks are you wearing?")
➡ **Lights:** Flashlights, the sun, emergency lights, etc., can cause a delay.

1. Examples of Sound to distract a person?

✓ Loud Scream of *NO! - STOP! - FIRE!*

2. Examples of Movement that would distract a person?

✓ Placing your hand in front of someone's face
✓ Covering their eyes
✓ Bobbing and weaving
✓ Running or jumping
✓ Looking behind a person
✓ Stomping your foot on the ground

3. Examples of a Psychological distraction?

✓ Asking an off-the-wall question:
  → "Do you know how to bake chocolate chip cookies?"
  → "When was the last time you bought socks?"

4. Examples of Light that would distract a person?

✓ Moving to a position where the sun or any type of light is in their eyes
✓ Shining a high-powered flashlight into a person's eyes
✓ Emergency vehicle lights

Learning to use time and distance can keep you safe, unhurt and alive in instances of workplace violence.

Chapter 10: Escape Planning

Developing escape plans for your various environments prepares you for the unfortunate event that you may need to escape from in a dangerous situation. This preparation is not intended to make you scared or paranoid, but to prepare you for the unexpected.

"Prepare for the worst, hope for the best, and expect some surprises along the way."

- David Fowler, author and creator of AVADE® Training

The first thing is to learn where all the exits are, in all environments you're in. It's a habit that could save your life. But not only are physical escapes needed, so are quick verbal responses that detach you from potential situations that can be negative, threatening and potentially dangerous or embarrassing.

"He who fails to plan, plans to fail."
- Proverb Quote

_____

"Planning is bringing the future into the present so that you can do something about it now."

– Alan Lakein, author of *How to Get Control of Your Time and Your Life*

Flashlight

Developing Escape Plans:

- **Own the Door**
- **Dominant Hand**
- **Proper Positioning**
- **Approach 45' Angle**
- **Spatial Empathy**
- **Proper Escorts**
- **Relationships**

Having an awareness of your exits in all environments is a highly encouraged habit that should be developed.

Own the Door

The concept of "own the door" is to not allow others between you and the door (your escape route) when dealing with individuals, who are in crisis; i.e. angry, highly stressed, recently terminated, intoxicated or combative. Position yourself so that you can escape if the situation becomes uncomfortable or dangerous. The environmental design of a facility can be limiting, but your awareness of your escape routes is the most important. With multiple individuals (visitors/guests/family members) in a room, politely ask them to all move to the furthest side of the room away from the doorway.

Improper Positioning

The best defense is to not be there when the attack takes place (avoidance), but if your escape route is compromised your last resort may be to defend yourself from an imminent attack. Always position yourself with an escape route in mind.

When multiple individuals are in a room (visitors, guests, family members), politely ask them to all move to the furthest side of the room away from the doorway.

Improper Positioning

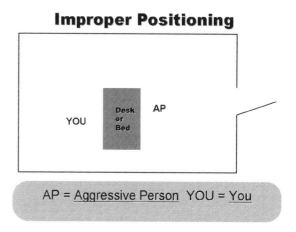

AP = Aggressive Person YOU = You

Staff whose office space is structured in such a way as this picture should:

1. Avoid dealing with difficult situations/people in your office.

2. If unavoidable (upset person just walks in), have a plan-use a distraction techniques to get out of your office and then confront individual in hallway or open space where available escape routes exist.

Dominant Hand / Proper Positioning

If a person becomes combative, they will more than likely strike you with their dominant hand. Positioning yourself on their dominant side makes it more difficult for them to strike at you. When dealing with at-risk individuals, position yourself on the dominant side of them.

Proper Positioning

You are always safer when you're at a 45-degree angle to a person who is upset. When standing, approaching, providing service to upset individuals and escorting individuals, use a 45-degree angle. This position is less threatening than facing them face to face, is a de-escalation technique and is the safest position for you to be in.

- Safe = 45 degrees in front of individual
- Safest = 45 degrees behind individual
- Unsafe = directly in front of an individual

Distance from the individual is also a major component of proper positioning.

"Spatial Empathy" is an informal term used to describe the awareness of an individual to the proximity, activities and comfort of people around them. Having spatial empathy means that you are aware of your personal zones, and the personal zones of other people around you. Having awareness that being in other people's personal zones may make them uncomfortable allows you to better serve, and be safer.

Proper Escort is used for individuals in crisis. The ABCs of proper escort are:

A. **Have the individual walk in front of you.**

B. **Maintain a 45-degree angle to them with proper distance.**

C. **Use your verbal and non-verbal skills to direct them where you want them to go.**

D. **Do not point with finger (use open hand)**

E. **Maintain your awareness**

Relationship Escape Plans refers to determining your escape route ahead of time in relation to the people you are around or come in contact with.

Developing Escape Plans

When it comes to developing escape plans, keep in mind the following:

Commitment: You must look at all your environments and pre-plan your escape routes. Saying you'll do it tomorrow turns into someday, which turns into no follow-through.

Involvement: Management should ensure that all staff know the plan. When discussing plans with staff, management should be serious and matter-of-fact. The leadership role when advising departmental staff members should be confident and free of emotional fear.

Practice: Just like your kids do fire drills at school, you should physically and mentally run through the events of your escape. Have a schedule and practice routinely.

"What if?" Game: The "What if?" Game means playing mental scenarios of situations that may arise and force us to take action. The best emergency responders and police officers play the "What if?" game regularly.

Changes: Realize now that things are going to change. You are going to change, and so are most things in life. With this said, doesn't it make sense to update your escape plans as your life changes?

Environments: Environmental Awareness means that you have an understanding of the different types of vulnerabilities and resilience your surroundings have or don't have.

Relationships: Escape planning always involves more than its physical nature. Successful personal safety involves communication skills that enable us to escape situations involving interpersonal relationships. A sharp awareness is keen to the sharp tongue.

Chapter 11: Environmental Factors

"You are a product of your environment. So choose the environment that will best develop you toward your objective. Analyze your life in terms of its environment. Are the things around you helping you toward success—or are they holding you back?"

- W. Clement Stone, Successful American Entrepreneur and Best-Selling Author (1902-2002)

Environments are a combination of external physical conditions that affect and influence the growth, development, and survival of organisms.

Workers move through many environments, even if they only work in one department. From parking lots, to cafeterias, corridors and lobbies, environments are unique in their associated risks. Environmental safety measures are put in place in workplaces to assist staff in protecting their environments, limiting access to their environments, and alerting others to assist them.

The following environmental safety measures are in place in multiple areas of the corporate and healthcare environment. Obviously, the higher risk areas require additional safety measures, however, all staff, regardless of their position, have access and a potential need for many of the safety measures.

The following environmental safety measures are in place in multiple areas of the workplace environment: The Environmental Safety Measures are in place to assist staff in protecting their environments, limiting access to their environments and alerting others to assist them.

Environmental Safety Measures:

1. Safety Mirrors
2. Lighting
3. Cameras – CCTV
4. Panic Alarms
5. Private Places
6. Access Controls
7. Staff Identification
8. Parking Lot Safety
9. Obstacles Around You
10. Telephone Safety

Safety Measure # 1 - Safety Mirrors

You use **mirrors** every day in your vehicle to keep yourself safe and aware of what's around you. If available, use the safety mirrors in your environment to alert you of obstacles, threats, and so that you can yield to guests and visitors.

Safety Measure # 2 - Lighting
"Criminals don't like lights"

It's an age-old axiom. Good lighting can discourage prowling or loitering. Always park and walk in areas with adequate lighting: entryways, pathways and stairwells.

Safety Measure # 3 – Cameras—CCTV

Closed circuit television allows you to see what is happening in different areas of your department, or in the entire workplace. It also helps the security/surveillance department to monitor from a remote location.

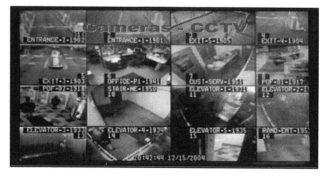

CCTV is great deterrent against criminals; however, if no one is watching at the moment an incident happens, no responders will be alerted. CCTV then becomes a tool for retrieving video after the fact.

Some panic alarm systems are connected to a central security dispatch center. When activated, the camera in that immediate area pops up on their monitor. But not all security systems have this in place.

Safety Measure # 4 – Panic Alarms

A panic or monitored alarm sends a signal to a remote location alerting them (usually security) to a breach in your security. These devices are mainly silent and are mounted in inconspicuous areas (under desk tops, etc.). Proper training and education on using alarms is essential to their use. Alarms should be regularly tested for their efficiency. Many key chains/fobs have a remote panic button that activates an audible alarm in the vehicle. This can be beneficial in parking lots and residences. Criminals are distracted by loud noises that alert and draw attention.

Safety Measure # 5 - Private Places to avoid: Stairwells & Elevators, Restrooms, etc.

Avoid using isolated, unused stairways in your environment. When using elevators, stand near the control panel by the door so you can easily press the alarm button in an emergency. If a suspicious-looking person follows you into an elevator, step out of the elevator immediately. If you see a suspicious-looking person inside an elevator you are about to enter, do not get in. If you are in an elevator and another person makes you feel uncomfortable, get off as soon as possible. Trust your instincts! Restrooms can isolate a person and compromise their escape route. If private restrooms are unavailable, lock doors, check stalls before entering, lock stall doors, and trust your instincts.

Safety Measure # 6 – Access Controls (door locks)

Access controls are designed to keep people out of specific areas. Memorize codes, be aware of who is around you when entering a locked area, and do not give codes or access to anyone who is unauthorized to be in the particular area. Be cautious of "piggy backing"— when someone enters an accessed area right after an authorized person has entered, following them in without approved access.

- **Security systems are only as good as the people using them.**
- **Learn how to use your security system properly.**

Safety Measure # 7 – Staff Identification

These days, most employees are required to wear a visible ID with their name and the area or department they work in. This ensures that access control is maintained as well as specific protocols for areas that are at a higher risk (cash vaults, administrative areas, staff only restrooms etc.).

Safety Measure # 8 – Parking Lot Safety

Parking lots, loading docks, blind alleys and trash container areas are prime crime points.
Most common crimes in these areas:

o Theft and Physical Assault

If possible, travel to and from work and parking areas with other people. Always park in areas that are patrolled and well-lit after dark and use security escorts during off-hours when others are not around

Also keep in mind:

✓ **Lighting:** Always choose well-lighted parking areas. Be aware of your surroundings!

✓ **Don't Sit:** Don't loiter in the parking lot. Take care of phone calls and other matters inside the location you are going to. Always turn off the ignition, remove the key, and lock your car doors, no matter how soon you plan on returning.

✓ **Valuables:** Keep valuables and packages locked in the trunk. If you are carrying packages, try to keep one hand free, even if it means making an extra trip.

✓ **Approaching:** Be alert as you approach your car in the parking area. Pay attention to nearby vehicles, individuals and hiding areas that criminals might use, such as under the car or in the back seat. Your keys and cell phone should be in hand or at reach. Always look around before you get in or out of your car.

✓ **Buddy System:** Always walk in groups when possible. Safety in numbers!

✓ **Security Escort:** Get a security escort if available.

✓ **Who's next to you?** Assess who you are next to when parking your car, and when coming back to your vehicle. If possible, do not park next to vans, trucks with campers or other vehicles whose size and structure can provide concealment for a potential assailant.

✓ **Parking Garages:** Exercise caution and be extra alert when using underground or enclosed parking garages. Walk in the center aisle, rather than close to parked cars. If you have a choice, park in areas that have an attendant, or in locations that have heavy pedestrian traffic. Have your key in hand before you get to your car and be aware of occupied cars around you.

Safety Measure # 9 – Obstacles Around You

The corporate and healthcare environment is filled with numerous obstacles that can inhibit your ability to escape a situation. Some common obstacles that can be trip hazards are chairs, people, walls, tables, cars, curbs, trees, inclement weather, machines, desks, spills on the floor etc.

Obstacles Around You

Safety Measure # 10 – Telephone Safety—Telephones & Emergency #'s

Cell Phones: Cell phones are a great tool for alerting others in almost every environment. Program numbers into your cell phone so that they are easily found and used. Some agencies use mass alert text messaging.

Threatening Calls: If you receive a threatening, harassing or obscene telephone call, notify security or police, your supervisor, and the telephone company.

Keep Records: Keep a record of the date, time and the content of each threatening, harassing or obscene telephone call for security or police and the telephone company. In some cases, cell phone companies can block callers who are threatening and harassing.

Emergency Numbers (What are yours?): Memorize numbers for emergency codes, police, security, fire, etc. Post the numbers near every telephone or on your person. Follow "Emergency Codes" response protocols.

Practice Emergency Numbers: Rehearse mentally and physically (turn phone off when practicing) calls you would make to police, fire, emergency personnel or anyone who would respond to your situation. Considering your stress level response, this skill could save your life.

ICE = In Case of Emergency: Program your cell phone with ICE numbers should you be unable to make a call yourself. Multiple ICE numbers can be added to your cell phone address book. Label them as ICE-1, ICE-2 etc.

Emergency Phones: Emergency phones can alert security personnel to your situation. Blue emergency phones are commonly found in parking structures and lots.

Consider all these factors when thinking about how your work environment will contribute to your safety, or make you unsafe. Also, consider some of the simplest things: your workplace is filled with numerous obstacles that can inhibit your ability to escape a situation. Some common obstacles that can be trip hazards are chairs, people, walls, tables, cars, curbs, trees, inclement weather, machines, desks, spills on the floor, etc. Be aware of changes in your environment that might inhibit your ability to escape a potentially violent incident.

Chapter 12: Emergency Codes & Procedures

> *"Be Prepared... the meaning of the motto is that a scout must prepare himself by previously thinking out and practicing how to act on any accident or emergency so that he is never taken by surprise."*
>
> - Sir Robert Baden-Powell, British Army Officer, founder of the Boy Scouts (1857-1941)

The use of codes is intended to convey essential information quickly, and with a minimum of misunderstanding to staff, while preventing stress or panic among guests and visitors to the workplace. Emergency codes are frequently coded by color, and the color codes denote different events at different corporations and are not always universal.

Plain language is also used to denote different types of emergencies. Know you emergency codes and responses!

This chapter is presented with the intent to prepare individuals in the workplace for emergent situations. The common emergencies in private corporations and healthcare include, but are not limited to: Fire, Medical, Hazmat, Bomb Threat, Lost Person, Robbery, Combative Person, Active Shooter and Personal Codes for Alerting Others.

Your corporate policies and procedures should be adhered to when responding to the following emergency situations.

Fire Code provides an appropriate response in the event of an actual or suspected fire in order to protect life, property and vital services.

Medical Code provides an appropriate response to a suspected or imminent medical emergency for a guest or staff person.

Hazmat Code provides an appropriate response to an actual or suspected hazardous material spill or release in a manner that is safe for staff, guests and visitors.

Bomb Threat Code provides an appropriate response in the event of a bomb threat or the discovery of a suspicious device/package.

Lost Person Code (Infant Abduction) provides an appropriate response in the event a lost person or possible child abduction from the facility.

Characteristics of an Abductor

The following is particular to health care facilities facing infant abductions: Listed below are characteristics of a typical abductor as identified by the National Center for Missing and Exploited Children (NCMEC). However, there is no guarantee an infant abductor will fit this description, and anyone acting suspicious in areas of risk for abductions should be reported immediately.

- Female of "childbearing" age (range from 12-50), often overweight.

- Most likely compulsive; most often relies on manipulation, lying, and deception.

- Frequently indicates that she has lost a baby or is incapable of having one.

- Often married or cohabitating; companion's desire for a child or the abductor's desire to provide her companion with "his" child may be the motivation for the abduction.

- Usually lives in the community where the abduction takes place.

- Frequently initially visits the nursery and maternity units at more than one healthcare facility prior to the abduction; asks detailed questions about procedures and the maternity floor layout; frequently uses a fire exit stairwell for escape; and may also try to abduct from the home setting.

- Usually plans the abduction, but does not necessarily target a specific infant; frequently seizes on any opportunity present.

- Frequently impersonates a nurse or other allied childcare personnel.

- Often becomes familiar with staff, staff work routines, and the victim's parents.

- Demonstrates a capability to provide "good" care to the baby once the abduction occurs.

- May remove the newborn as follows: carrying the infant, carrying a bag large enough to hold an infant, covering the infant with coat/baby blanket, or may be in healthcare/childcare uniform/scrubs carrying the infant.

Robbery Code provides an appropriate response in the event of an armed or unarmed robbery. Businesses that handle money, deal with prescription pharmaceuticals or sell high-end items are at risk of a robbery.

AVADE® Robbery Prevention & Response Guidelines

Robbery is the crime of seizing property through violence or intimidation. A perpetrator of a robbery is a robber. Because violence is an ingredient of most robberies, they may result in the harm or murder of their victims.

Robbers want your money or property, and they want it quickly. Robbery is a risky business and robbers are usually nervous. You do not want to delay a robbery in any way—it increases the potential for violence. Give the robber what he or she wants and do it quickly. Do not risk your life, or another person's life, for property.

Robberies occur at predictable times. Opening and closing periods are particularly vulnerable times due to low staffing and large amounts of cash on hand. Robberies increase during the holiday season due to the increased cash volume, and the presence of large crowds that distract and preoccupy store and company personnel.

Report suspicious activity. If you observe an individual(s), or occupied vehicle, lingering around your business for a time, or in a manner that makes you suspicious or uncomfortable, write down the license number, color and make of the car, description of the individual(s) and call police or security. Many robbers like to watch and wait for the right opportunity.

PREVENTION - Security Devices

(See Chapter 12: Environmental Factors)

- Control access to areas where cash or other valuable items are stored.
- CCTV is a great deterrent against criminals.
- Signage inside and outside will emphasize your security policy on limited cash on hand and/or employee inaccessibility to the safe.
- Silent "hold-up" or "panic" alarms should be considered.

PREVENTION - Identification

Greet each customer. Establish eye contact and remember their general appearance. Good customer service discourages hesitant robbers as well as other thieves. This attention to detail conveys control and puts people on notice they have been observed and can be identified later.

Place height markings along the vertical frame at the entrance. This gives employees the ability to tell how tall the robber is at a glance, so they can tell the authorities.

PREVENTION - Policy Considerations

Recognize your potential for being held up. Work with local police and crime prevention specialists. Preventive strategies are as much their concern and responsibility as apprehension of criminals.

- Check references of prospective employees. Do a background check of their previous employers.
- Keep a file on all employees, including their pictures. Past employees know store procedure and where money is kept.
- Re-key locks, and reset codes and combinations when affected employees are dismissed for cause.
- Establish clear and consistent policies regarding money in the till. Establish how much money will be kept in the till, what bill denominations employees will accept, how to respond to "suspicious" inquires, and how to handle loiterers. All employees should be trained and given a written description of store policy.
- Maintain adequate staff levels. Be especially careful during opening and closing periods, lunch hours, and holiday seasons, when there is more money on-site and more distractions.
- As an employee, your commitment to security procedures will reduce the risk of criminal confrontation and physical harm.

PREVENTION - Design Considerations

- Use gates and counters to separate clients from employees when appropriate.
- Post signs to designate restricted areas: "Private" or "Employees Only."
- Install an information desk and staff it during business hours. It will provide some surveillance of the main entrance of the building.
- Create transition zones. These can be steps up or down, screened or partitioned off areas, different levels of lighting or carpeting in a given space. These methods subtly indicate a change in usage from public to private.

- Report any broken lights, flickering lights, broken locks or doors, dimly lit corridors, doors that don't lock properly, broken windows, or lock devices to management or security immediately. Not attending to these items can create an environment conducive to crime. The faster they are repaired the safer the environment will be.

PREVENTION - Business Security Procedures

Develop company security procedures. The procedures should state the company's policy and dedication to a crime-and-violence-free workplace. Including procedures for the following will help empower employees to make their workplace safe and crime-free.

- Dealing with trespassers and/or difficult people
- Opening and closing the office
- Using the office during off hours
- Recommendations for personal property security
- Who to report crimes and suspicious activities to
- Emergency exit plan

Robbery Prevention

When to Call Emergency Numbers:

- A crime is in progress
- A situation is about to escalate into an emergency (endangering life or major property)
- A crime has just occurred (remember description of suspect and direction in which he or she fled)

Be Alert Pay attention to who is in your work area, and know who belongs in your work area. Become familiar with the faces of people who belong in your building. Pay attention to people who behave suspiciously, i.e. someone who loiters in the area with no apparent purpose. Be particularly aware of a person you have seen loitering more than once.

Response During the Robbery

- Remain calm. Most robbers do not wish to harm their victims. They are only interested in getting money or property. The calmer you are, the less chance that the robber becomes agitated or dangerous. This also increases your chances of getting a more accurate description of the robber, which may aid in the robber's apprehension.

- Do not argue, fight, surprise or attempt to use weapons against a robber. He has already taken a major risk by entering your business and is usually as frightened as you are. Because of this, additional provocation on your part could make the situation worse. Therefore, give the robber exactly what he or she wants and do it quickly. Don't take unnecessary chances with your life!

- While you should cooperate with robbers, don't volunteer any assistance. Don't give all the money if the robber only asks for twenty-dollar bills.

- Activate silent alarms/security devices if you can do this without detection.

- Watch the robber's hands. If the robber is not wearing any gloves, anything he touches might leave good fingerprints.

- Give the robber your "bait" money. Be sure to inform the investigating officer that you did so.

- Be systematic in your observations. Look the robber over carefully. Mentally note as many details as possible until you can write them down. Compare the robber with yourself. Is he taller, heavier, older, etc.

- Notice the type and description of any weapons used. Glance at the weapon only long enough to identify it. Look at the robber from then on. Make no sudden moves and don't be heroic!

- Observe the direction the robber takes in leaving the scene. If a vehicle is involved, make note of the make, model, year, color, license plate number and issuing state.

Response After the Robbery

- Telephone police immediately. If you act quickly, police might be able to catch the suspect and recover your money. When you dial 9-1-1, the procedure is always the same. You will be asked if your emergency involves police, fire or medical. Request police.

- Lock all doors and allow no one in. Ask witnesses to remain on the premises until police arrive. Do not touch anything the robber may have touched. Do not discuss what happened with any other witnesses. Your own impressions should be kept untainted until you have talked with authorities.

- Complete your post-incident documentation. Be as complete as possible. Police may want a copy of your report. (See Chapter 7 for post incident documentation procedures.)

- Provide incident debriefing. (See Chapter 8 for critical incident stress debriefing.)

Robbery response strategies require planning and coordination between employees and management. Give some thought to how you might react in a robbery situation and discuss your concerns with co-workers and employers. Common sense, caution and adherence to established policies and procedures can reduce the amount of money stolen and minimize the chance for injury and loss of life.

Combative Person Code

Combative Person Code provides an appropriate response to situations involving an aggressive/hostile/combative or potentially combative person.

Note: ***Early Warning Signs*** (See Chapter 6 Combative Person Signs & Symptoms)

To avoid a threatening or escalated response by the aggressive individual proper positioning of the team is crucial. Team cornering of an aggressive individual may escalate the situation.

Contact and Cover Positioning

Level III Defensive Control Tactics and Techniques covers team response to a combative person known as "Contact and Cover."

- It is critically important when having to confront and control a combative person that you **DO NOT** surround or corner them. Proper positioning is crucial. Contact and Cover is the main strategy in the defensive control tactics and techniques.

Combative Person Team Positioning

Contact and Cover Positioning

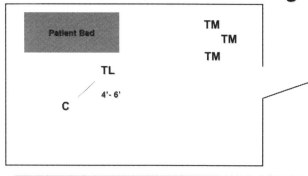

CP = Combative Person   TL = Team Leader
TM = Team Members

Contact and Cover Positioning

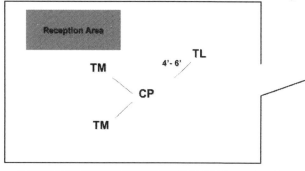

CP = Combative Person   TL = Team Leader
TM = Team Members

Active Shooter Code

Active Shooter Code provides an appropriate response in the event of an incident involving a person brandishing or using a weapon.

Active Shooter (Awareness-Preparedness & Response)

Active Shooter Defined

An **active shooter** is an individual actively engaged in killing or attempting to kill people in a confined and other populated area. In most cases, **active shooters** use firearms and there is no pattern or method to their selection of victims.

Responses to Active Shooter
1. Armed Response – Law Enforcement
2. Unarmed Response – Escape!

The most extreme incidence of violence in today's society is an active shooter event. Active Shooter incidents take place in a variety of environments.

Environmental Awareness for Active Shooter Incidents

➡ **Malls**
➡ **Schools**
➡ **Hospitals**
➡ **Churches**
➡ **Restaurants**
➡ **Medical Clinics**
➡ **Movie Theatres**
➡ **Sporting Events**
➡ **Military Installations**
➡ **Government Buildings**
➡ **Retail Shops and Stores**

According to the Federal Bureau of Investigation:
- 160 Active Shooter incidents occurred between 2000 and 2013
- An average of 11.4 incidents occurred annually, with an increasing trend from 2000 -2013
- 1,043 casualties, including killed and wounded:
- 486 were killed in 160 incidents
- 557 were wounded in 160 incidents

Active Shooter Situations are unpredictable, evolve quickly, and continue until stopped by: law enforcement, suicide, or intervention.

What we know about Active Shooters

- The active shooter is acting alone 98% of the time.

- He is suicidal 90% of the time, and usually commits suicide onsite.

- He almost never takes hostages, nor has any interest in negotiating.

- Is preoccupied with a high body count, which is almost always his one and only goal.

- Active-shooters race to murder everybody they reach in an effort to avoid contact with police. Most incidents are over within 4-8 minutes or less!

- Shooter usually has multiple weapons & an ability to reload his weapons several times.

- Long arms (rifles/shotguns) are involved 80% of the time.

- High prediction of serious injury to the innocent and unarmed.

- At least 50% of the time, the person stopping the incident is non-police.

Active Shooter Characteristics

Active Shooters are motivated by:

- ➡ **Anger**
- ➡ **Ideology**
- ➡ **Religion**
- ➡ **Revenge**
- ➡ **Retaliation**
- ➡ **Mental Illness**
- ➡ **Media Stardom**

Surviving An Active Shooter

1. Escape if safe to do so!
2. Hide and cover in place if you cannot escape. (SAFE ROOM)
3. Alert authorities—police, security.
4. Locks doors in your immediate area.
5. Place barriers and remain absolutely quiet.
6. If escape is not possible and danger is imminent, attack the attacker.
7. When law enforcement arrives, go face down on ground with palms up.

Escape if safe to do so # 1

- Have an escape route & plan in mind
- Leave your belongings behind
- Help others escape, if possible
- Evacuate regardless of others
- Warn/prevent individuals from entering
- Do not attempt to move wounded people

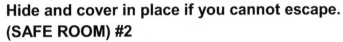

Hide and cover in place if you cannot escape. (SAFE ROOM) #2

- **Your hiding spot should:**
- Be out of the active shooter's view
- Provide protection if shots are fired
- Not restrict options for movement

Alert authorities—police, security. #3

- **Provide Law Enforcement or 911 operators with:**
    - Location of shooter(s)
    - Number of shooters
    - Physical description of shooter(s)
    - Number and types of weapons
    - Number of potential victims
    -

Locks doors in your immediate area. #4

If the shooter is nearby:
- Lock the door
- Hide behind large item (cabinet, desk)
- Silence cell phone/pager
- Remain quiet

Place barriers and remain absolutely quiet. #5

If escape is not possible and danger is imminent, attack the attacker.
#6 As an absolute last resort:

- Act as aggressively as possible
- Improvise weapons and throw items
- Yell and Scream!
- Commit to your actions

Awareness and vigilance play the most important role in overall prevention and intervention of violence. When faced with imminent danger, one must realize that mental strength will be absolutely necessary to stay alive and survive.

When law enforcement arrives, go face down on ground with palms up. #7
Law Enforcements Role in an Active Shooter Situation

Law Enforcements Immediate purpose:
- Stop the active shooter!
- Proceed to area where last shots heard
- First priority is to eliminate the threat

Police Entry Teams may:
- Wear bulletproof vests, helmets, and other tactical equipment
- Be armed with rifles, shotguns, and/or handguns
- Shout verbal commands!
- Push individuals to the ground for their safety

When Law Enforcement Arrives:
- Remain calm and DO what they tell YOU!
- Put down any items in your hands
- Raise hands and spread fingers
- Avoid quick or sudden movements
- Avoid pointing, screaming, or yelling
- Proceed in direction from which officers are entering

Go to a Safe Location!
Area controlled by law enforcement until:
- The situation is under control
- All witnesses are identified and questioned
- They release you to leave area

See Run-Hide-Fight Video:
https://www.fbi.gov/about-us/office-of-partner-engagement/active-shooter-incidents/run-hide-fight-video

Personal Codes for Alerting Others

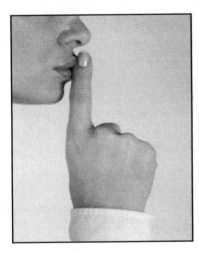

Personal Codes for Alerting Others provide a quick, non-attention-getting communication to security or other responders of a possible threatening, emergent or imminent situation. Using personal codes between team members can alert help without alerting the assailant that you are requesting assistance/help.

Conclusion
Workplace violence is, unfortunately, on the rise. But by studying the AVADE® strategies, learning them, integrating them and teaching them to your co-workers, you can lessen your chances of being a victim of workplace violence.

Learn the AVADE® principles for defusing tense situations. Learn to identify the signs and symptoms of potential violence. Above all, learn to trust your instincts, and listen to your intuition. Remember: your best tool for keeping yourself safe is your own mind.

NOTES

AVADE® Level II
Self-Defense Tactics and Techniques

The Goal of Self-Defense

The goal of this section is to teach self-defense intervention tactics and techniques. Most incidents can be prevented using your awareness, vigilance and avoidance. However, there may be times when you need to physically intervene to protect yourself or another person. **After any self-defense intervention, always escape and report immediately.** Before conducting any physical training be sure to cover the following safety rules with your class. Safety is the most important rule in physical training.

In today's society, corporations, healthcare, schools, gaming, law enforcement, security, corrections, military and protective services agencies realize that self-defense tactics and techniques are essential for protecting themselves and the public that they serve. These agencies also understand that mitigating liability begins with proper training and education in self-defense tactics and techniques.

The **AVADE®** training program is designed for agencies to reduce the potential of injury and liability risk when lawfully defending themselves or controlling an aggressive individual. The tactics and techniques in this training curriculum are for incidents where the aggressor is physically combative, resistive and unarmed*.

This training manual, provides training and education that is designed to empower individuals, increase awareness, knowledge, skills and actions with regard to use of force, control and restraint, self-defense, and defending others with self-defense tactics and techniques.

This course stresses the importance of knowing your agency policies and procedures in regard to using force and defending yourself or another person. The **AVADE®** training is intended to give the trainee the basic understanding of self-defense, use of force, control and restraint, reasonable force and basic legal definitions of force. **Personal Safety Training Inc.** makes no legal declaration, representation or claim as to what force should be used or not used during a self-defense, use of force incident or assault incident or situation. Each trainee must take into consideration their ability, agency policies and procedures and laws in the state and country in which they reside

The techniques in this training course are uncomplicated for most individuals to learn and develop proficiency. Basic self-defense fundamentals are taught followed by defensive blocking techniques, personal defensive weapons, vulnerable areas of the body, specific responses to holds-assaults and post incident response and documentation procedures.

First Rule of Training = Safety

Before taking part in any physical training YOU must understand the safety rules.

- **Weapons Free environment:** No weapons are allowed anywhere in the training area. Instructor will advise participants in proper procedures in securing weapons and ammunition. Follow agency policy and procedures.

- **Remove jewelry, etc.:** The following should not be worn during a class which involves hands-on training: all jewelry with sharp edges; pins or raised surfaces; or jewelry that encircles the neck.

- **No Horseplay Rule:** Any participant who displays a disregard for SAFETY to anyone in class will be asked to leave the class. Please practice only the technique currently being taught. **DO NOT PRACTICE UNAUTHORIZED TECHNIQUES**

- **Pat out Rule (used for control techniques):** Upon hearing/feeling/seeing the "PAT," your partner applying the technique will immediately release the pressure of the technique to reduce discomfort/pain. The technique will be immediately and totally released on instructions from the instructor or when a safety monitor says "RELEASE," "STOP," or words similar to them.

- **Be a Good, "Good Guy" and a "Good Bad Guy":** Essentially this means working together with your partner when practicing the techniques. Without cooperation while practicing self-defense or defensive control tactics techniques, time is wasted and injury potential is increased. Work together to learn together!

- **Check equipment for added safety:** The instructor will check all equipment used during the training to ensure proper function, working order and safety.

- **Practice techniques slowly at first:** Gain balance and correctness slowly before practicing for speed. Proceed at the pace directed by your trainer.

- **Advise instructor of ANY pre-existing injuries:** Any injury or condition that could be further injured or aggravated should be brought to the immediate attention of your instructor, and your partner, prior to participating in any hands-on training.

- **Advise instructor of ANY injury during class:** Any injury, regardless of what it is, needs to be reported to the primary instructor.

- **Safety is EVERYONE'S responsibility!:** Safety is everyone's responsibility and everyone is empowered to immediately report or YELL OUT any safety violation or concern about safety.

- **Training Hazards:** Always keep any items or training equipment and batons off the floor/ground and out of the way when not in use. They are potential tripping/fall hazards.

- **Safety Markings:** COLORED WRIST BANDS or RED/BLUE TAPE worn by any participant is the sign to warn of an injury. USE CAUTION WITH A PARTNER WHO IS WEARING A COLORED WRIST BAND OR RED/BLUE TAPE.

- **STRETCHING:** A low-impact stretching, from head to toe can prevent possible injuries and strains. Keep eyes open, avoid jerking and bouncing, and breathe.

What is Self-Defense

What is Self-Defense? Self-defense is the right to use <u>reasonable</u> force to protect one's self or members of one's staff/family from bodily harm from the attack of an aggressor, if you have reason to believe that you or they are in danger.

Individuals do have the right to self-defense. The application must follow any agency policy and procedure as well as state and federal law. The best self-defense is to avoid the situation and get away. If avoidance and escape are not possible, a reasonable defense would be lawful as a last resort.

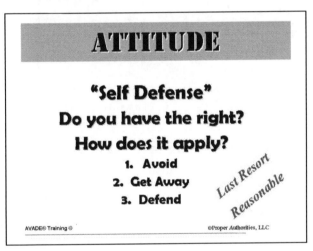

The following information will provide a general understanding of self-defense and use-of-force so that you can legally protect yourself against liability risks associated with any type of self-defense and/or use-of-force.

> ### Disclaimer
> This section is intended to give the trainee the basic understanding of self-defense, use of force and reasonable force. Personal Safety Training Inc. makes no legal declaration, representation or claim as to what force should be used or not used during a self-defense, use of force incident, or assault incident or situation. Each trainee must take into consideration their ability, agency policies and procedures and laws in the state and country in which they reside.

Self-Defense Fundamentals

Fundamentals of Self-Defense

Every tactic and technique requires the understanding and use of fundamental laws. If the fundamental law is absent or lacking, the individual's ability to defend himself is compromised. A basic understanding and use of these laws will give you the advantage in a situation where you will need to use force to defend yourself or another person.

Fun·da·men·tal

(from the Latin medieval: *fundāmentālis*: belonging to a foundation. 1400-50, late Middle English.

—*Synonyms* 1. Indispensable, primary.

–adjective

1. Serving as, or being an essential part of, a foundation or basis; basic; underlying: *fundamental principles; the fundamental structure.*
2. Of, pertaining to, or affecting the foundation or basis: *a fundamental revision.*
3. Being an original or primary source: *a fundamental idea.*

–noun

1. A basic principle, rule, law, or the like, that serves as the groundwork of a system; essential part: *to master the fundamentals of a trade.*
2. Also called fundamental note, fundamental tone. *Music.*
3. *The* root of a chord.
4. The generator of a series of harmonics.
5. *Physics,* The component of lowest frequency in a composite wave.

Self-Defense Fundamentals

- **Stance-Balance-Stability**
- **Defensive Movements**
- **Core Energy Principle**
- **Defense Verbalization**
- **Distraction Techniques**
- **Escape Strategies**
- **Reactionary Gap**
- **Hand Positions**

The Bladed (defensive) Stance

The Bladed (defensive) Stance

➧ All techniques in the self-defense tactics training are performed from the bladed stance.

Objective

➧ Demonstrate how to correctly position your body to protect your vulnerable line and maintain stance, balance and stability.

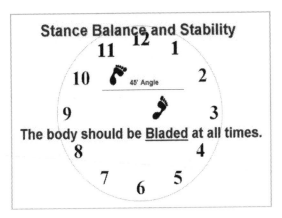

Performance—Bladed Stance

➧ Face the clock (diagram on PowerPoint or imagine a clock in front of you) with your feet shoulder-width apart.

1. Step straight back with either left or right foot. Usually individuals prefer to have their dominant foot to the rear.

2. If you stepped back with your right foot, turn your feet and body to the one o'clock position.

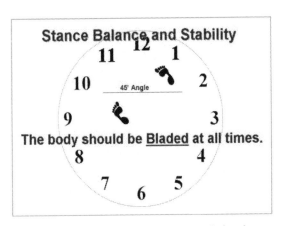

3. If you stepped forward with your left foot, turn your feet and body to the eleven o'clock position.

4. Keep your weight equal on both feet, and your knees slightly bent.

Performance Stability Test (Bladed Stance)

1. Partner exercise (A & B)

2. Partner A places his/her feet together. Partner B gently pushes partner A to the front, back, left side and right side. Reverse roles.

3. Partner A stands with his/her feet should width apart. Partner B gently pushes partner A to the front, back, left side and right side. Reverse roles.

4. Partner A now assumes the bladed stance. Partner B gently pushes partner A to the front, back, left side and right side. Reverse roles.

The Bladed Stance protects your "Vulnerable Line" away from the subject.

Defensive Movements—Forward Shuffle

Forward movement is used to engage a subject for control or defense.

Forward Shuffle

This Defensive movement involves being able to move forward while maintaining balance and stability. All defensive tactics techniques are enhanced with defensive movement.

Objective

Demonstrate how to correctly move forward.

Performance—Forward Movement

1. Assume the bladed stance.
2. Take a short step forward with your front foot (shuffle).
3. Follow up with a short step forward using your rear foot.
4. Continue forward, using forward shuffling movement.

Caution: If the feet come together, balance and stability are compromised (common mistake).

The rule of defensive movement is:

The foot that is closest to the direction you want to go, always moves first.

Defensive Movements—Rear Shuffle

Rear movement is used to disengage from an aggressor.

Rear Shuffle

This Defensive movement involves being able to move to the rear (backwards) while maintaining balance and stability. All defensive tactics techniques are enhanced with defensive movement.

Objective

Demonstrate how to correctly move to the rear.

Performance—Rear Movement

1. Assume the bladed stance.
2. Take a short step to back with the rear foot (shuffle).
3. Follow up with a short step back using your front foot.
4. Continue backwards, using rear shuffling movement.

Caution: If the feet come together, balance and stability are compromised (common mistake).

Caution: Back pedaling is another common mistake.

Caution: Obstacles in your environment.

The rule of defensive movement is:

The foot that is closest to the direction you want to go, always moves first.

Defensive Movements—Side to Side Shuffle

Side to side movement is used to avoid an attack from an aggressor.

Side to Side Shuffle
This Defensive movement involves being able to move side to side while maintaining balance and stability. All defensive tactics techniques are enhanced with defensive movement.

Objective
Demonstrate how to correctly move side to side

Performance—Side-to-Side Movement

1. Assume the bladed stance.
2. Take a short step to the right using your right foot.
3. Follow up with a short step to the right using your left foot.
4. Take a short step to the left using your left.
5. Follow up with a short step to the left using your right foot.

Caution: If the feet come together, balance and stability are compromised (common mistake).

Caution: Crossing feet up is another common mistake.

Caution: Obstacles in your environment.

The rule of defensive movement is:
The foot that is closest to the direction you want to go, always moves first.

Defensive Movements—Forward & Rear Pivoting

Pivoting is used to reposition or to enhance your energy when using personal defensive weapons or defensive control tactics

Forward & Rear Pivoting

This Defensive movement involves being able to pivot forward or back while maintaining balance and stability. All defensive tactics techniques are enhanced with defensive movement.

Objective

Demonstrate how to correctly pivot forward and backward.

Performance—Pivoting (forward and back)

1. Assume the bladed stance.
2. Take an arcing step forward with your rear foot (forward pivot).
3. Take an arcing step backward with your front foot (rear pivot).
4. When pivoting forward or backward, always remain balanced and stable.
5. Pivots can be small movements or up to a 360 degree pivot.

Caution: If the feet come together, balance and stability are com promised (common mistake).

Caution: Crossing feet up is another common mistake.

Caution: Obstacles in your environment.

Robot Exercise (The Best Self-Defense Technique!)

Defensive Movement "Robot Exercise"

The robot exercise involves being able to move in a lateral motion (side to side) to avoid an attack that us coming at you from a distance of 4' away or greater.

Objective

Demonstrate how to correctively avoid a forward attack by moving out of the way.

Performance—Robot Exercise

1. Defender assumes a bladed defensive stance.
2. From 4-6" away the attacker places hands out directly toward the defender.
3. Attacker moves forward toward the defender, attempting to gently touch either shoulder of the defender.
4. Defender waits for last moment to move to either side

   away from attack.
5. Using sounds and/or movements will assist defender in distracting the attacker.
6. Once out of the attack zone, defender can proceed to keep moving away from the attacker.

Caution: Do not move too late!

Caution: Do not move too soon or attacker will have time to adjust (reaction time) and follow/track you.

Caution: Crossing feet up is another common mistake.

Caution: Beware of obstacles in your environment.

Core Energy Principle

Core Energy

Our central and most essential part of our strength and power is our core energy. Without core energy we rely on our extremities which are not as strong as our central core. All defensive tactics techniques utilize this essential principle.

Having Core Energy will:

✓ Give YOU advantage over subjects.

✓ Provide YOU power for counter blocks/defenses.

✓ Help the YOU better control and decentralize a physically resistive subject.

Objective

Demonstrate how to correctly use your core energy.

Performance—Core Energy

1. Partner exercise (A & B)

2. Partner A faces partner B with his/her elbows away from their core.

3. Partner B moves forward toward partner A. Partner A pushes partner B back by pushing at their shoulders. How did it go? Reverse roles.

4. Partner A again, faces partner B with his/her elbows down towards their core.

5. Partner B moves forward toward partner A. Partner A pushes partner B back by pushing at their shoulders. How did it go? Reverse roles.

Defensive Verbalization

During all Defenses: Use loud repetitive Defensive Verbalizations

➡ NO!
➡ STOP!
➡ GET BACK!
➡ LET ME GO!
➡ LEAVE ME ALONE!

Defensive Verbalization:
Creates witnesses
Establishes authority
Keeps YOU breathing
May be used a distraction
Alerts other of a confrontation
Provides direction to the aggressor
Mitigates liability risk to YOU and your agency

The Art of Distraction

Is a process by which we buy valuable time to **Escape, Defend** or **Control.**

Sounds (Loud Scream/Yell) - Movements – Psychological - Lights

Distractions affect the senses which take time for the mind to process the new information. They mainly affect a person's sight and sense of hearing; however, psychological distractions such as asking a person something completely out of the ordinary can cause a mental delay as well. Distractions have been used since ancient times and are a valuable advantage you should always use.

Sounds: Using a loud scream or yell can cause a momentary delay.

Movements: Using your hands, eyes, and body can distract and cause a momentary delay.

Psychological: Asking a person something completely out of the ordinary can cause them a mental delay.

Lights: Flashlights, the sun, emergency lights, etc., can cause a delay.

Escape Strategies

- Escape is the act or instance of breaking free from danger or threat, or from being trapped, restrained, confined or isolated against your will.
- Planning is the cognitive process of thinking about what you will do in the event of something happening.

Reactionary Gap

The Reactionary Gap is 4-6 Feet. "Action beats Reaction with-in the Reactionary Gap"
The distance between and individual and an agressoe in which the ability to react is impaired due to the close proximity of the agressor.

Hand Positions

There are six basic defensive hand positions.

Objective
Demonstrate how to correctly use your hands in the stop, caution, defensive, authoritative, directive and open positions.

Performance—<u>Stop or Caution</u> Hand Positions
1. Assume the bladed stance
2. Position your arms with your elbows down and your palms facing outward.
3. The non-verbal message says "don't come close to me," or a non-threatening message if you're moving forward.

Performance—<u>Defensive or Authoritative</u> Hand Positions
1. Assume the bladed stance
2. Position your arms with your elbows down and you palms in a bladed position.
3. Position your arms with your elbows down and your palms down.
3. The nonverbal message is defensive or authority.

- **Caution:** Closing your hands into a fist position may send a message of aggression.

Performance—<u>Directive or Open</u> Hand Positions
1. Assume the Bladed Stance
2. Position your arms and hands pointing with your hand in the direction you want someone to go.
3. Position your arms with your elbows down and your palms facing upward.

- **Caution:** Do not point when giving directions, as pointing is perceived as a derogatory gesture.

Shoulder Block Defense

Shoulder Block Defense
Is a technique that teaches individuals how to deflect an imminent assault.

Objective
Demonstrate how to properly use a defensive shoulder block against a physical assault to your head.

Performance—Shoulder Block Defense
1. Assume the bladed stance.
2. Bring your chin down.
3. Drop the arm that is in front of you while bringing your shoulder up to your chin.
4. You can slightly rotate your body towards your back side as the assault comes towards you, further deflecting the attack.

During all Defenses:
- Use loud defensive verbalizations (NO, STOP, GET BACK, LEAVE ME ALONE, etc.) to direct the aggressor to stop attacking you.
- Use defensive movements (Escape!)

After all Defenses:
- Follow agency policies and procedures in regard to self-defense.
- Report and Document immediately.

Elbow Block Defense

Elbow Block Defense
Is a technique that teaches individuals how to deflect an imminent assault.

Objective
Demonstrate how to properly use a defensive elbow block against a physical assault to your head.

Performance—Elbow Block Defense
1. Assume the bladed stance.
2. Bring your chin down.
3. Bring your front arm up to your face with your elbow directly in front, creating a shield in front of your face.
4. You can slightly rotate your body towards your back side as the assault comes towards you, further deflecting the attack.

During all Defenses:
- Use loud defensive verbalizations (NO, STOP, GET BACK, LEAVE ME ALONE, etc.) to direct the aggressor to stop attacking you.
- Use defensive movements (Escape!)

After all Defenses:
- Follow agency policies and procedures in regard to self-defense.
- Report and Document immediately.

Turtle Block Defense

Turtle Block Defense

Is a technique that teaches individuals how to deflect an imminent assault.

Objective

Demonstrate how to properly use a defensive turtle block against a physical assault to your head and torso.

Performance—Turtle Block Defense

1. Assume the bladed stance.
2. Bring your chin down.
3. Bring both arms up in front of your face with your elbows directly in front, creating a shield in front of your and body face.
4. You can slightly rotate your body towards your back side as the assault comes towards you, further deflecting the attack.

During all Defenses:

- Use loud defensive verbalizations (NO, STOP, GET BACK, LEAVE ME ALONE, etc.) to direct the aggressor to stop attacking you.
- Use defensive movements (Escape!)

After all Defenses:

- Follow agency policies and procedures in regard to self-defense.
- Report and Document immediately.

High Block Defense

High Block Defense
Is a technique that teaches individuals how to deflect an imminent assault to your head.

Objective
Demonstrate how to properly use a defensive high block against a physical assault to your head.

Performance—High Block Defense

1. Assume the bladed stance.
2. Bring your chin down.
3. Bring your arm up in front of your face with your palm out.
4. Your hands can be open or closed.
5. You can use your support arm, strong arm or both arms to defend against an attack to your head.

During all Defenses:
- Use loud defensive verbalizations (NO, STOP, GET BACK, LEAVE ME ALONE, etc.) to direct the aggressor to stop attacking you.

- Use defensive movements (Escape!)

After all Defenses:
- Follow agency policies and procedures in regard to self-defense.
- Report and Document immediately.

Middle Block Defense

Middle Block Defense

Is a technique that teaches individuals how to deflect an imminent rushing assault or grappling attack towards you.

Objective

Demonstrate how to properly use a defensive middle block against a physical assault coming at you.

Performance—Middle Block Defense

1. Assume the bladed stance.
2. Bring both arms up in front of you (palms out).
3. Push the aggressor away at the shoulders or torso area.
4. Use side-to-side movement after the middle block defense to get into a position of advantage or to continue to defend.

During all Defenses:

• Use loud repetitive defensive verbalizations (NO, STOP, GET BACK, LEAVE ME ALONE,

• etc.) to direct the aggressor to stop attacking you.

• Use defensive movements (Escape!)

After all Defenses:

• Follow agency policies and procedures in regard to self-defense.

• Report and Document immediately.

Outside Block Defense

Outside Block Defense
Is a technique that teaches individuals how to deflect an imminent assault to either side of your body.

Objective
Demonstrate how to properly use a defensive outside block against a physical assault coming to either side of your body.

Performance—Outside Block Defense
1. Assume the bladed stance.
2. Bring either your right or left (or both) up arms in front of your body and pivot towards the direction of the attack.
3. Your hands can be open or closed.
4. You can use your support arm, strong arm or both arms to defend against an attack to either side of your body.

During all Defenses:
• Use loud defensive verbalizations (NO, STOP, GET BACK, LEAVE ME ALONE, etc.) to direct the aggressor to stop attacking you.
• Use defensive movements (Escape!)

After all Defenses:
• Follow agency policies and procedures in regard to self-defense.
• Report and Document immediately.

Low Block Defense

Low Block Defense
Is a technique that teaches individuals how to deflect an imminent attack to lower area of the body.

Objective
Demonstrate how to properly use a defensive low block against a physical assault coming to the lower part of your body.

Performance—Low Block Defense
1. Assume the bladed stance.
2. Bring either your right or left (or both) arm down, sweeping in front of your body and moving the attack away.
3. Your hands can be open or closed.
4. You can use your support arm, strong arm or both arms to defend against an attack to the lower area of your body.

During all Defenses:
- Use loud defensive verbalizations (NO, STOP, GET BACK, LEAVE ME ALONE, etc.) to direct the aggressor to stop attacking you.
- Use defensive movements (Escape!)

After all Defenses:
- Follow agency policies and procedures in regard to self-defense.
- Report and Document immediately.

Palm Heel Defense

Palm Heel Defense
The palm heel defense counter strike may be a reasonable defense from an attack of an aggressor.

Objective
Demonstrate how to correctly use a palm heel defense technique to defend against an attack from an aggressor.

Performance—Palm Heel Defense
1. Assume the bladed stance.
2. Position your strong or support hand with your heel extended outward.
3. Fingers are in a claw position and have nothing to do with the defense.
4. You can pivot your body forward thrusting your heel into the desired area of impact.

During all Defenses:
- Use loud defensive verbalizations (NO, STOP, GET BACK, LEAVE ME ALONE, etc.) to direct the aggressor to stop attacking you.
- Use defensive movements (Escape!)

After all Defenses:
- Follow agency policies and procedures in regard to self-defense.
- Report and Document immediately.

Fist Defense

Fist Defense

The fist defense counter strike may be a reasonable defense from an attack of an aggressor.

Objective

Demonstrate how to correctly use a fist defense technique to defend against an attack from an aggressor.

Performance—Fist Defense

1. Assume the bladed stance.
2. Position your strong or support hand with your fingers clenched tightly into your palm.
3. Vertical or horizontal fist positions can be used.
4. You can pivot your body forward thrusting your fist into the desired area of impact.

Caution: Proper fist position is required to avoid injuring yourself.

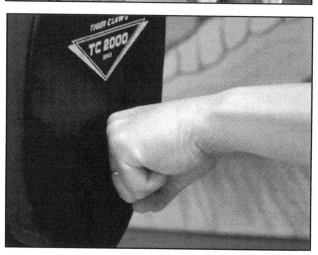

During all Defenses:
- Use loud defensive verbalizations (NO, STOP, GET BACK, LEAVE ME ALONE, etc.) to direct the aggressor to stop attacking you.
- Use defensive movements (Escape!)

After all Defenses:
- Follow agency policies and procedures in regard to self-defense.
- Report and Document immediately.

Hammer Fist Defense

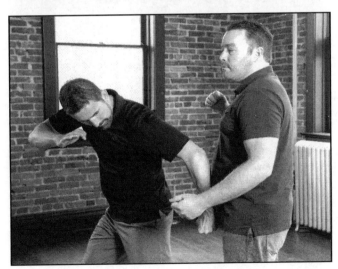

Hammer Fist Defense
The hammer fist defense counter strike may be a reasonable defense from an attack of an aggressor.

Objective
Demonstrate how to correctly use a fist defense technique to defend against an attack from an aggressor.

Performance—Hammer Fist Defense
1. Assume the bladed stance.
2. Position your strong or support hand with your fingers clenched tightly into your palm.
3. Vertical, diagonal or horizontal hammer fist
defenses may be used.
4. You can pivot your body forward thrusting your fist into the desired area of impact.

Caution: Proper fist position is required to avoid injuring yourself.

During all Defenses:
- Use loud defensive verbalizations (NO, STOP, GET BACK, LEAVE ME ALONE, etc.) to direct the aggressor to stop attacking you.
- Use defensive movements (Escape!)

After all Defenses:
- Follow agency policies and procedures in regard to self-defense.
- Report and Document immediately.

Forearm Defense

Forearm Defense
The forearm defense counter strike may be a reasonable defense from an attack of an aggressor.

Objective
Demonstrate how to correctly use a forearm defense technique to defend against an attack from an aggressor.

Performance—Forearm Defense
1. Assume the bladed stance.
2. Position your strong or support hand with your fingers clenched tightly or in an open position.
3. Vertical, diagonal or horizontal forearm defenses may be used.
4. You can pivot your body forward or backward thrusting your forearm into the desired area of impact.

During all Defenses:
- Use loud defensive verbalizations (NO, STOP, GET BACK, LEAVE ME ALONE, etc.) to direct the aggressor to stop attacking you.
- Use defensive movements (Escape!)

After all Defenses:
- Follow agency policies and procedures in regard to self-defense.
- Report and Document immediately.

Elbow Defense

Elbow Defense
The elbow defense counter strike may be a reasonable defense from an attack of an aggressor.

Objective
Demonstrate how to correctly use an elbow defense technique to defend against an attack from an aggressor.

Performance—Elbow Defense
1. Assume the bladed stance.
2. When using your strong/support hand elbow, you can blade your hand or clenched hand tightly.
3. Vertical, frontal and rear elbow defenses may be used.
4. You can pivot your body forward or backward thrusting your elbow into the desired area of impact.

During all Defenses:
- Use loud defensive verbalizations (NO, STOP, GET BACK, LEAVE ME ALONE, etc.) to direct the aggressor to stop attacking you.
- Use defensive movements (Escape!)

After all Defenses:
- Follow agency policies and procedures in regard to self-defense.
- Report and Document immediately.

Knee Defense

Knee Defense
The knee defense counter strike may be a reasonable defense from an attack of an aggressor.

Objective
Demonstrate how to correctly use a knee defense technique to defend against an attack from an aggressor.

Performance—Knee Defense
1. Assume the bladed stance.
2. Your support or strong knee can be used.
3. Your foot should be pulled back when defending, creating a pointed knee for impact.
4. You can pivot your body forward thrusting your knee into the desired area of impact.

During all Defenses:
- Use loud defensive verbalizations (NO, STOP, GET BACK, LEAVE ME ALONE, etc.) to direct the aggressor to stop attacking you.
- Use defensive movements (Escape!)

After all Defenses:
- Follow agency policies and procedures in regard to self-defense.
- Report and Document immediately.

Kick Defense

Kick Defense
The kick defense counter strike may be a reasonable defense from an attack of an aggressor.

Objective
Demonstrate how to correctly use a frontal and side kick defense technique to defend against an attack from an aggressor.

Performance—Frontal and Side Kick Defense
1. Assume the bladed stance.
2. Your support or strong side can be used for frontal and sidekicks.
3. For the frontal kick, your toes should be pulled back.
4. For the side kick use the edge of your outer foot.

Caution: Balance may be compromised when deploying a defensive kick.

During all Defenses:
• Use loud defensive verbalizations (NO, STOP, GET BACK, LEAVE ME ALONE, etc.) to direct the aggressor to stop attacking you.
• Use defensive movements (Escape!)

After all Defenses:
• Follow agency policies and procedures in regard to self-defense.
• Report and Document immediately.

NOTES

129

Vulnerable Areas of the Body

➡ Knowledge of self-defense is very important, but just as important is where and when you would deploy your defenses if/when necessary.

➡ Without this knowledge and understanding, your interventions could be ineffective or expose you to unnecessary liability risk.

➡ The "Vulnerable Areas" of the body diagrams denote lower, medium, and high-risk target areas.

Low Risk Target Areas

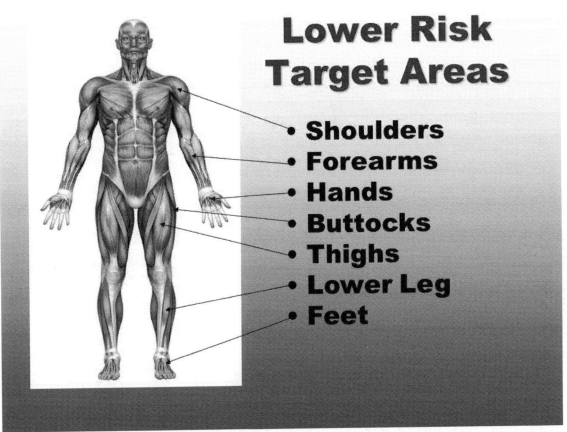

- Low Risk Target Areas are for situations where the subject is resisting/attacking an individual or another person.

- The subject's body would be considered low risk for the application of blocks and restraint techniques (excluding the Head, Neck and Spine).

- The level of resultant trauma to these areas tends to be minimal or temporary, yet exceptions may occur.

An individual/agency MUST always consider their policies and procedures, state and federal laws when using any force or self-defense interventions.

Medium Risk Target Areas

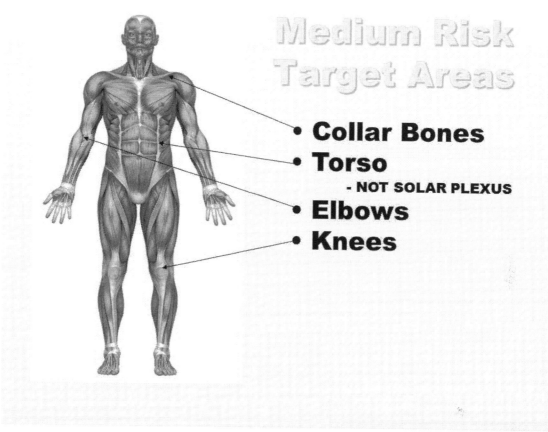

Medium Risk
Target Areas

- **Collar Bones**
- **Torso**
  - NOT SOLAR PLEXUS
- **Elbows**
- **Knees**

- Medium Risk Target Areas are for situations where the subject is resisting/attacking an individual or when force applied to a Low Risk Target Area fails to overcome the subject's resistance/attack.

- Medium Risk Targets are areas of the human body that include joints and areas that are in close proximity to a High Risk Target Area. Risk of potential injury is increased.

- The level of resultant trauma to these areas tends to be moderate to serious. Injury may last for longer periods of time, or may be temporary.

An individual/agency MUST always consider their policies and procedures, state and federal laws when using any force or self-defense interventions.

High Risk Target Areas

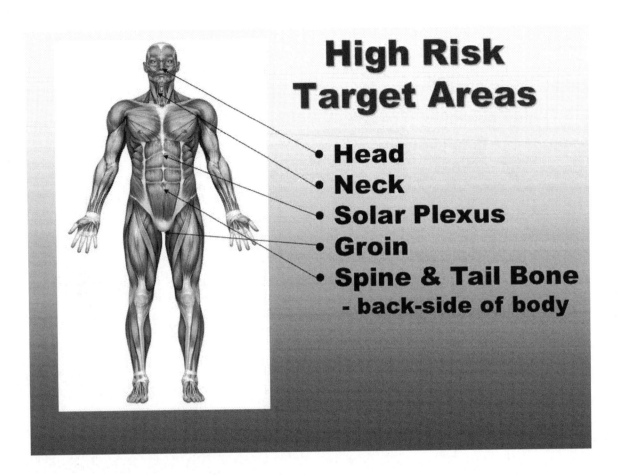

High Risk Target Areas

- **Head**
- **Neck**
- **Solar Plexus**
- **Groin**
- **Spine & Tail Bone**
  - **back-side of body**

- High Risk Target Areas are for situations where the subject is using force that is likely to cause serious injury or death to an individual or another person.

- Force directed to High Risk Target Areas may cause greater risk of injury to the subject. Individuals must be justified and reasonable in using deadly force against a subject.

- The level of resultant trauma to these areas tends to be serious and/or long lasting. Injury to subject may include: serious bodily injury, unconsciousness, shock or death.

An individual/agency MUST always consider their policies and procedures, state and federal laws when using any force or self-defense interventions.

Wrist Grab Defense

Wrist Grab Defense
Is a technique that teaches individuals how to defend themselves from a one-handed wrist grab assault.

Objective
Demonstrate how to defend against a one-handed wrist grab assault situation.

Performance—Wrist Grab Defense
1. Defender stabilizes after being grabbed by the wrist.
2. Defender pulls elbow into their core (or moves forward to get their elbow into their core).
3. Defender turns palm upward, grabbing their hand with their free hand.
4. Defender then pulls their hand upward, using their core energy to break free of the assault.
5. Defender may need to use a distraction technique or personal defensive weapon to break free from the assault.

During all Defenses:
- Use loud repetitive defensive verbalizations (NO, STOP, GET BACK, LET ME GO, LEAVE ME ALONE etc.) to direct the aggressor to stop attacking you.
- Use defensive movements (Escape!)

After all Defenses:
- Follow agency policies and procedures in regard to self-defense.
- Report and Document immediately.
-

Two-Hand Wrist Grab Defense

Two-Hand Wrist Grab Defense
Is a technique that teaches individuals how to defend themselves from a two-handed wrist grab assault.

Objective
Demonstrate how to defend against a two-handed wrist grab assault situation.

Performance—Two Hand Wrist Grab Defense
1. Defender stabilizes after being grabbed by the wrists.
2. Defender pulls both elbows into their core (or moves forward to get their elbows into their core).
3. Defender turns palms upward, while raising both hands upward in a circular outward motion to release the grab.
4. Defender may need to bring their palms back ward in a reverse circular motion to release the grab.
5. Defender may need to use a distraction technique or personal defensive weapon to break free from assault.

During all Defenses:
• Use loud repetitive defensive verbalizations (NO, STOP, GET BACK, LET ME GO, LEAVE ME ALONE etc.) to direct the aggressor to stop attacking you.
• Use defensive movements (Escape!)

After all Defenses:
• Follow agency policies and procedures in regard to self-defense.
• Report and Document immediately.

Front Choke Defense Exercise

Front Choke Defense
Is a technique that teaches individuals how to defend themselves from a frontal choke assault.

Objective
Demonstrate how to defend against a frontal choke assault situation.

Note: A front choke assault is done from close range, unless a person has you up against a wall or pinned to the floor.

Performance—Front Choke Defense
1. Defender stabilizes after being grabbed around the throat with both hands.
2. Defender can utilize a palm heel defense, knee defense, finger spears to the eyes, foot stomp, or any personal defense weapon.
3. Defender may need to use repeated defensive moves to break free from this assault.
4. This assault is potentially life threatening and defender will need to respond immediately to break free from the assault.

During all Defenses:
- Use loud repetitive defensive verbalizations (NO, STOP, GET BACK, LET ME GO, LEAVE ME ALONE etc.) to direct the aggressor to stop attacking you.
- Use defensive movements (Escape!)

After all Defenses:
- Follow agency policies and procedures in regard to self-defense.
- Report and Document immediately.

Front Choke Defense (Special Situation)

Front Choke Defense (Special Situation)

Is a technique that teaches individuals how to defend themselves from a frontal choke assault.

Objective

Demonstrate how to defend against a frontal choke assault situation.

Note: Typically a front choke assault is done from close range, unless a person has you up against a wall or pinned to the floor.

Performance—Front Choke Defense

1. Defender stabilizes after being grabbed around the throat with both hands, arms extended.
2. Defender can utilize a finger spear technique to the bottom of the throat/top of the rib cage of the attacker.
3. Finger spear is done by placing two fingers together and pushing in and down.
4. Defender may need to turn their body sideways if attacker's arms are long.
5. Defender may need to use other personal defense techniques.

During all Defenses:

- Use loud repetitive defensive verbalizations (NO, STOP, GET BACK, LET ME GO, LEAVE ME ALONE etc.) to direct the aggressor to stop attacking you.
- Use defensive movements (Escape!)

After all Defenses:

- Follow agency policies and procedures in regard to self-defense.
- Report and Document immediately.

Rear Airway Choke Defense

Rear Airway Choke Defense

Is a technique that teaches individuals how to defend themselves from a rear airway choke assault.

Objective

Demonstrate how to defend against a rear airway choke assault situation.

Note: A rear airway choke assault can compromise your ability to breathe and verbalize. Individuals will need to respond immediately to this type of assault.

Performance—Rear Airway Choke Defense

1. Defender stabilizes after being grabbed around the throat from behind.
2. Defender pulls attackers arm downward towards their core.
3. After core is established, defender will turn their head away from attackers elbow and place their palm under the attackers elbow.
4. Defender will then pivot and push attackers elbow into the air to escape the assault.
5. Defender may need to use personal defense weapons to escape assault.

During all Defenses:

- Use loud repetitive defensive (NO, STOP, GET BACK, LET ME GO, LEAVE ME ALONE etc.) to direct the aggressor to stop attacking you.
- Use defensive movements (Escape!)

After all Defenses:

- Follow agency policies and procedures in regard to self-defense.
- Report and Document immediately.

Rear Carotid Choke Defense

Rear Carotid Choke Defense
Is a technique that teaches individuals how to defend themselves from a rear carotid choke assault.

Objective
Demonstrate how to defend against a rear carotid choke assault situation.

Note: A rear carotid choke assault can compromise your ability to breathe, verbalize and may render unconsciousness. Individuals will need to respond immediately to this assault.

Performance—Rear Carotid Choke Defense
1. Defender stabilizes and immediately place fingers into their carotid neck areas and pulls downward to core.
2. Once stabilized, defender can bring their chin down and push up on the attackers elbow with same side hand.
3. This position pushes the elbow onto the chin of the de fender allowing defender to breathe.
4. Defender can bite the arm of the attacker and use the hand not at the elbow for defense weapon techniques.
5. Defense weapons are used for escape.

During all Defenses:
• Use loud repetitive defensive verbalizations (NO, STOP, GET BACK, LET ME GO, LEAVE ME ALONE etc.) to direct the aggressor to stop attacking you.
• Use defensive movements (Escape!)

After all Defenses:
• Follow agency policies and procedures in regard to self-defense.
• Report and Document immediately.

Rear Bear Hold Defense

Rear Bear Hold Defense
Is a technique that teaches individuals how to defend themselves from a rear bear hold assault.

Objective
Demonstrate how to defend against a rear bear hold assault situation.

Note: A rear bear hold assault can compromise your ability to breathe as well as being picked up and thrown down or taken to another location.

Performance—Rear Bear Hold Defense
1. Defender stabilizes and immediately grabs onto attackers hands and bends forward using core.
2. Once bent forward, defender launches their head back (head butt) into the face of the attacker.
3. Defender will head butt until arms are released.
4. Once arms are released, defender may elbow or use other personal defense weapons to break free from as sault.
5. Defense weapons are used for escape.

During all Defenses:
- Use loud repetitive defensive verbalizations (NO, STOP, GET BACK, LET ME GO, LEAVE ME ALONE etc.) to direct the aggressor to stop attacking you.
- Use defensive movements (Escape!)

After all Defenses:
- Follow agency policies and procedures in regard to self-defense.
- Report and Document immediately.

Ground Defenses

Ground Defenses
Is a technique that teaches individuals how to defend themselves from an attack where they have been thrown, hit or went to the ground voluntarily.

Objective
Demonstrate how to defend from a ground assault situation.

Performance—Ground Defenses
1. Defender immediately curls into a fetal position with their dominant side upward (preferably).
2. From this position the defender is protected and appears submissive.
3. Once attacker moves into to assault, the defender can launch a side kick defense just below the knee of the attacker.
4. The defender may need to rotate from one side to an other as attacker moves.
5. Defender should maintain awareness and vigilance when getting up off of the ground. Do not give up your backside!

Note: Attacker may have a knife/edged weapon making this a life threatening situation for the defender.

During all Defenses:
- Use loud repetitive defensive verbalizations (NO, STOP, GET BACK, LET ME GO, LEAVE ME ALONE etc.) to direct the aggressor to stop attacking you.
- Use defensive movements (Escape!)

After all Defenses:
- Follow agency policies and procedures in regard to self-defense.
- Report and Document immediately.

Gun Threat Response Defense

Gun Threat Response Defense
Is a technique that teaches individuals how to defend themselves against a gun threat response.

Objective
Demonstrate how to respond/defend from a gun threat.

Note: See "Active Shooter" response. If possible ESCAPE immediately

Performance—Gun Threat Response Defense
1. Defender immediately brings hands up to a non-threatening position.
2. Defender blocks the hand (same-side) holding the gun while turning (blading) their body.
3. Defender then grabs gun with free hand, bringing (pivot) it into the holstered position.
4. The attackers gun muzzle should be pointed upward with defenders forearm securing the attacker arm.
5. Defender may need to use personal defense weapons to immobilize the attacker. Attacker may end up on the ground.

Note: This is a life-threatening situation for the defender.

During all Defenses:
- Use loud repetitive defensive verbalizations (NO, STOP, GET BACK, LET ME GO, LEAVE ME ALONE etc.) to direct the aggressor to stop attacking you.
- Use defensive movements (Escape!)

After all Defenses:
- Follow agency policies and procedures in regard to self-defense.
- Report and Document immediately.

Knife Threat Response Defense

Knife Threat Response Defense
Is a technique that teaches individuals how to defend themselves against a knife threat response.

Objective
Demonstrate how to respond/defend from a knife threat.

Note: If possible ESCAPE immediately!

Performance—Knife Threat Response Defense
1. Defender immediately brings hands up to a non-threatening position.
2. Defender blocks the hand (same-side) holding the knife while turning (blading) their body.
3. Defender then grabs the hand with free hand, bringing (pivot) it into the holstered position.
4. The attacker's knife blade should be pointed upward with defenders forearm securing the attacker arm.
5. Defender may need to use personal defense weapons to immobilize the attacker. Attacker may end up on the ground.

Note: This is a life threatening situation for the defender.

During all Defenses:
- Use loud repetitive defensive verbalizations (NO, STOP, GET BACK, LET ME GO, LEAVE ME ALONE etc.) to direct the aggressor to stop attacking you.
- Use defensive movements (Escape!)

After all Defenses:
- Follow agency policies and procedures in regard to self-defense.
- Report and Document immediately.

Elements of Reporting Self-Defense or Force

Report and Document
After any situation involving defense of yourself or another person, proper documentation and reporting is crucial. The events of the assault or attempted assault should be reported to security/police. The police/security will document the incident and start an investigation. You should also document the account for your own internal records. This can protect you in a possible legal situation that could arise out of using force to defend yourself. As you document your account of the incident make sure to report to security/police any details you missed during your initial report to them.

What type of force/self-defense was used during the incident?
Be specific in your documentation regarding the type of control, defense and force that was used during the incident.

How long did the incident and resistance last?
Important to note the length of the resistance, as this is a factor relative to exhaustion and increasing the level of force.

Was any de-escalation used?
Verbal and non-verbal de-escalation techniques should be noted.

Were you in fear of injury (bodily harm) to yourself, others or the subject?
Fear is a distressing emotion aroused by perceived threat, impending danger, evil or pain.

If so, Why?
Fear is a basic survival mechanism occurring in response to a specific stimulus, such as pain or the threat of danger.

Thoroughly explain, and make sure to document completely.
The importance of documentation cannot be over emphasized. Documentation ensures proper training standards are met, policies and procedures are understood, certification standards are met, liability and risk management mitigation, and departmental and organizational requirements are maintained. A ruling in the United States, Whiteley v. Warden, 410 U.S. 560 (1971), states, that if it is not documented (training and the incident specifics), it did not happen. Therefore, if you do not document your training, a court may rule that training did not occur.

Special Note
Every person must take into consideration their moral, legal and ethical beliefs, rights and understandings when using any type of force to defend themselves or others. **Personal Safety Training Inc.** makes no legal declaration, representation or claim as to what force should be used or not used during a self-defense/assault incident or situation. Each trainee must take into consideration their ability, agency policies and procedures and state and federal laws.

Civilian Levels of Defense

- **Awareness-Vigilance-Avoidance:** As we learned in modules 1-3, the best defense is to be aware, use your vigilance and avoid conflicts. This is the base of the chart and the most important aspect of defense.

- **Confident Presence:** Our presence can be a major deterrent against predators. Using confident postures, facial expressions and eye communication shows that we are not an easy target.

- **Interpersonal Communications Skills:** When faced with people who are stressed, angry, intoxicated, or combative, your best initial defense is your ability to communicate. See Module 4.

- **Escape Options:** When faced with a situation that is escalating and dangerous, if possible you should escape to a safe location and alert others.

- **OC Pepper Spray:** Pepper sprays are a non-lethal force option which can distract the predator, giving you time to escape or defend.

- **Personal Defensive Weapons:** Include unarmed defenses such as, your bodies, hands, feet and self-defense escape techniques.

- **Personal Defense Tools:** Non-lethal items which you can use in your hands to defend yourself. Examples: key chains, umbrellas, flashlights, rolled up newspaper, etc.

- **Deadly Defense:** Defense against what you believe to be serious injury and or death to you by a person(s) using a deadly weapon or assaulting you.

Static Air and Blocking Drills

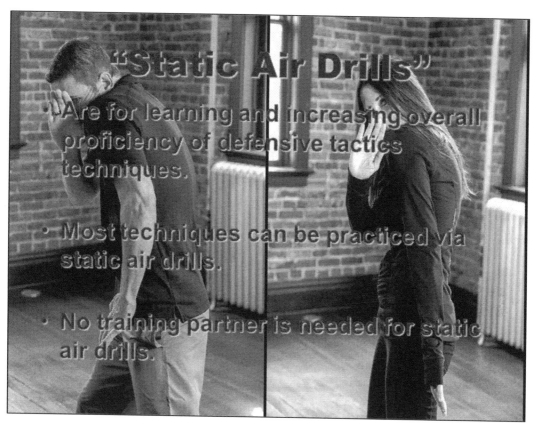

"Static Air Drills"
- Are for learning and increasing overall proficiency of defensive tactics techniques.
- Most techniques can be practiced via static air drills.
- No training partner is needed for static air drills.

"Blocking Drills"
- Are for learning and increasing overall proficiency of the blocking techniques.
- Partners, plastic wiffel ball bats, foam batons or impact bags can be used to increase realism.
- Blocking drills are dynamic and motivate personnel.

Impact and Partner Drills

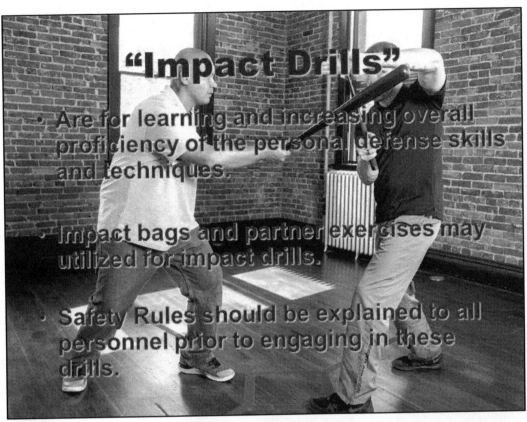

"Impact Drills"

- Are for learning and increasing overall proficiency of the personal defense skills and techniques.

- Impact bags and partner exercises may utilized for impact drills.

- Safety Rules should be explained to all personnel prior to engaging in these drills.

"Partner Drills"

- Increases overall proficiency of defensive tactics techniques.

- All techniques can be practiced via partner drills except for striking unless YOU are using the appropriate safety gear.

- Partner drills create realism and are engaging to personnel.

Positioning and Combination Drills

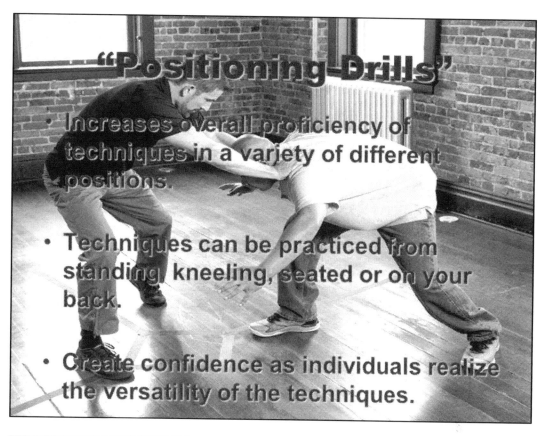

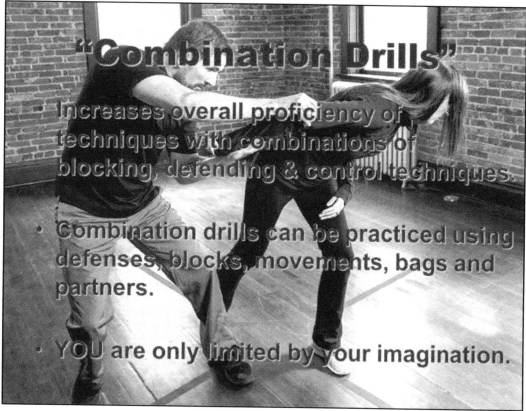

AVADE® Level III

Defensive Control Tactics and Techniques

Introduction to the Defensive Control Tactics and Techniques

The goal of this section is to teach defensive control tactics and techniques. Most incidents can be prevented using your awareness, vigilance and avoidance. However, there may be times when you need to physically control a subject who is out of control and a risk to themselves or others.

- After any control tactics and techniques, always follow post incident responses and documentation procedures.
- Before conducting any physical training be sure to cover the following safety rules with your class. Safety is the most important rule in physical training.

In today's society, corporations, healthcare, schools, gaming, law enforcement, security, corrections, military and protective services agencies realize that defensive control tactics and techniques are essential for protecting themselves and the public that they serve. These agencies also understand that mitigating liability begins with proper training and education in defensive control tactics strategies and techniques.

The **AVADE**® training program is designed for agencies to reduce the potential of injury and liability risk when lawfully defending themselves or controlling an aggressive individual. The tactics and techniques in this training curriculum are for incidents where the aggressor is physically combative, resistive and unarmed.

This training manual, provides training and education that is designed to empower individuals, increase awareness, knowledge, skills and actions with regard to use of force, control and restraint, self-defense, and defending others with defensive control tactics strategies and techniques.

This course stresses the importance of knowing your agency policies and procedures in regard to using force and defending yourself or another person. The **AVADE**® training is intended to give the trainee the basic understanding of self-defense, use of force, control and restraint, reasonable force and basic legal definitions of force. **Personal Safety Training Inc.** makes no legal declaration, representation or claim as to what force should be used or not used during a self-defense, use of force incident or assault incident or situation. Each trainee must take into consideration their ability, agency policies and procedures and laws in the state and country in which they reside

The techniques in this training course are uncomplicated for most individuals to learn and develop proficiency. Basic defensive tactics fundamentals are taught followed by contact and cover positioning, escort strategies & techniques, control & decentralization, prone and supine restraint and post incident response and documentation procedures.

First Rule of Training = Safety

Before taking part in any physical training YOU must understand the safety rules.

- **Weapons Free environment:** No weapons are allowed anywhere in the training area. Instructor will advise participants in proper procedures in securing weapons and ammunition. Follow agency policy and procedures.

- **Remove jewelry, etc.:** The following should not be worn during a class which involves hands-on training: all jewelry with sharp edges; pins or raised surfaces; or jewelry that encircles the neck.

- **No Horseplay Rule:** Any participant who displays a disregard for SAFETY to anyone in class will be asked to leave the class. Please practice only the technique currently being taught. **DO NOT PRACTICE UNAUTHORIZED TECHNIQUES**

- **Pat out Rule (used for control techniques):** Upon hearing/feeling/seeing the "PAT," your partner applying the technique will immediately release the pressure of the technique to reduce discomfort/pain. The technique will be immediately and totally released on instructions from the instructor or when a safety monitor says "RELEASE," "STOP," or words similar to them.

- **Be a Good, "Good Guy" and a "Good Bad Guy":** Essentially this means working together with your partner when practicing the techniques. Without cooperation while practicing self-defense or defensive control tactics techniques, time is wasted and injury potential is increased. Work together to learn together!

- **Check equipment for added safety:** The instructor will check all equipment used during the training to ensure proper function, working order and safety.

- **Practice techniques slowly at first:** Gain balance and correctness slowly before practicing for speed. Proceed at the pace directed by your trainer.

- **Advise instructor of ANY pre-existing injuries:** Any injury or condition that could be further injured or aggravated should be brought to the immediate attention of your instructor, and your partner, prior to participating in any hands-on training.

- **Advise instructor of ANY injury during class:** Any injury, regardless of what it is, needs to be reported to the primary instructor.

- **Safety is EVERYONE'S responsibility!:** Safety is everyone's responsibility and everyone is empowered to immediately report or YELL OUT any safety violation or concern about safety.

- **Training Hazards:** Always keep any items or training equipment and batons off the floor/ground and out of the way when not in use. They are potential tripping/fall hazards.

- **Safety Markings:** COLORED WRIST BANDS or RED/BLUE TAPE worn by any participant is the sign to warn of an injury. USE CAUTION WITH A PARTNER WHO IS WEARING A COLORED WRIST BAND OR RED/BLUE TAPE.

- **STRETCHING:** A low-impact stretching, from head to toe can prevent possible injuries and strains. Keep eyes open, avoid jerking and bouncing, and breathe.

Use of Force

Any use of force or self-defense intervention must be reasonable and legally justified.

Awareness of "LIABILITY RISK"

When any force is used, the individual MUST take into consideration their ability, agency policies and procedures and laws in the state and country in which they reside.

Unauthorized or inappropriate use of force or defense may expose the individual and/or agency to criminal and/or civil liability.

Personal Safety Training Inc. does not dictate policies or procedures for arrest, detention, control and restraint, self-defense, use of force or any physical intervention authorized for use by a department/agency or private individual. The suggestions, options and techniques disseminated during this training program are simply that, suggestions, options and techniques. Each individual, department or agency is responsible for developing their own "policies and procedures" regarding use of force, self-defense, physical intervention, physical restraints, physical control, arrest and detention for their personnel.

What are YOUR policies and procedures for use of force and self-defense?

Individuals (staff) MUST have a strong understanding of their agency policies and procedures regarding use of force and self-defense.

Defensive Control Tactics Fundamentals

Fundamentals of Defensive Control Tactics

Every tactic and technique requires the understanding and use of fundamental laws. If the fundamental law is absent or lacking, the individual's ability to defend/control is compromised. A basic understanding and use of these laws will give you the advantage in a situation where you will need to use force to control someone, defend yourself or another person.

Fun·da·men·tal

(from the Latin medieval: *fundāmentālis*: belonging to a foundation. 1400-50, late Middle English.

—Synonyms 1. Indispensable, primary.

–adjective

1. Serving as, or being an essential part of, a foundation or basis; basic; underlying: *fundamental principles; the fundamental structure.*
2. Of, pertaining to, or affecting the foundation or basis: *a fundamental revision.*
3. Being an original or primary source: *a fundamental idea.*

–noun

1. A basic principle, rule, law, or the like, that serves as the groundwork of a system; essential part: *to master the fundamentals of a trade.*
2. Also called fundamental note, fundamental tone. *Music.*
3. *The* root of a chord.
4. The generator of a series of harmonics.
5. *Physics,* The component of lowest frequency in a composite wave.

Defensive Control Tactics Fundamentals

- **Stance-Balance-Stability**
- **Defensive Movements**
- **Core Energy Principle**
- **Defense Verbalization**
- **Distraction Techniques**
- **Escape Strategies**
- **Reactionary Gap**
- **Hand Positions**

The Bladed (defensive) Stance

The Bladed (defensive) Stance

➡ All techniques in the self-defense tactics training are performed from the bladed stance.

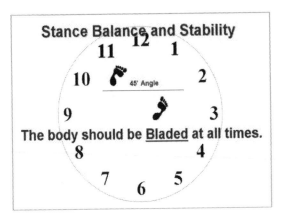

Objective

➡ Demonstrate how to correctly position your body to protect your vulnerable line and maintain stance, balance and stability.

Performance—Bladed Stance

➡ Face the clock (diagram on PowerPoint or imagine a clock in front of you) with your feet shoulder-width apart.

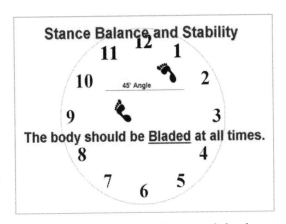

1. Step straight back with either left or right foot. Usually individuals prefer to have their dominant foot to the rear.

2. If you stepped back with your right foot, turn your feet and body to the one o'clock position.

3. If you stepped forward with your left foot, turn your feet and body to the eleven o'clock position.

4. Keep your weight equal on both feet, and your knees slightly bent.

Performance Stability Test (Bladed Stance)

1. Partner exercise (A & B)

2. Partner A places his/her feet together. Partner B gently pushes partner A to the front, back, left side and right side. Reverse roles.

3. Partner A stands with his/her feet should width apart. Partner B gently pushes partner A to the front, back, left side and right side. Reverse roles.

4. Partner A now assumes the bladed stance. Partner B gently pushes partner A to the front, back, left side and right side. Reverse roles.

The Bladed Stance protects your "Vulnerable Line" away from the subject.

Defensive Movements—Forward Shuffle

Forward movement is used to engage a subject for control or defense.

Forward Shuffle

This Defensive movement involves being able to move forward while maintaining balance and stability. All defensive tactics techniques are enhanced with defensive movement.

Objective

Demonstrate how to correctly move forward.

Performance—Forward Movement

1. Assume the bladed stance.
2. Take a short step forward with your front foot (shuffle).
3. Follow up with a short step forward using your rear foot.
4. Continue forward, using forward shuffling movement.

Caution: If the feet come together, balance and stability are compromised (common mistake).

The rule of defensive movement is:
The foot that is closest to the direction you want to go, always moves first.

Defensive Movements—Rear Shuffle

Rear movement is used to disengage from an aggressor.

Rear Shuffle
This Defensive movement involves being able to move to the rear (backwards) while maintaining balance and stability. All defensive tactics techniques are enhanced with defensive movement.

Objective
Demonstrate how to correctly move to the rear.

Performance—Rear Movement
1. Assume the bladed stance.
2. Take a short step to back with the rear foot (shuffle).
3. Follow up with a short step back using your front foot.
4. Continue backwards, using rear shuffling movement.

Caution: If the feet come together, balance and stability are compromised (common mistake).

Caution: Back pedaling is another common mistake.

Caution: Obstacles in your environment.

The rule of defensive movement is:
The foot that is closest to the direction you want to go, always moves first.

Defensive Movements—Side to Side Shuffle

Side to side movement is used to avoid an attack from an aggressor.

Side to Side Shuffle

This Defensive movement involves being able to move side to side while maintaining balance and stability. All defensive tactics techniques are enhanced with defensive movement.

Objective

Demonstrate how to correctly move side to side

Performance—Side-to-Side Movement

1. Assume the bladed stance.

2. Take a short step to the right using your right foot.

3. Follow up with a short step to the right using your left foot.

4. Take a short step to the left using your left.

5. Follow up with a short step to the left using your right foot.

Caution: If the feet come together, balance and stability are

compromised (common mistake).

Caution: Crossing feet up is another common mistake.

Caution: Obstacles in your environment.

The rule of defensive movement is:

The foot that is closest to the direction you want to go, always moves first.

Defensive Movements—Forward & Rear Pivoting

Pivoting is used to reposition or to enhance your energy when using personal defensive weapons or defensive control tactics

Forward & Rear Pivoting
This Defensive movement involves being able to pivot forward or back while maintaining balance and stability. All defensive tactics techniques are enhanced with defensive movement.

Objective
Demonstrate how to correctly pivot forward and backward.

Performance—Pivoting (forward and back)
1.   Assume the bladed stance.
2.   Take an arcing step forward with your rear foot (forward pivot).
3.   Take an arcing step backward with your front foot (rear pivot).
4.   When pivoting forward or backward, always remain balanced and stable.
5.   Pivots can be small movements or up to a 360 degree pivot.

Caution: If the feet come together, balance and stability are com promised (common mistake).

Caution: Crossing feet up is another common mistake.

Caution: Obstacles in your environment.

Robot Exercise (The Best Self-Defense Technique!)

Defensive Movement "Robot Exercise"
The robot exercise involves being able to move in a lateral motion (side to side) to avoid an attack that us coming at you from a distance of 4' away or greater.

Objective
Demonstrate how to correctively avoid a forward attack by moving out of the way.

Performance—Robot Exercise
1. Defender assumes a bladed defensive stance.
2. From 4-6" away the attacker places hands out directly towards the defender.
3. Attacker moves forward toward the defender, attempt-
   ing to gently touch either shoulder of the defender.

4. Defender waits for last moment to move to either side away from attack.
5. Using sounds and/or movements will assist defender in distracting the attacker.
6. Once out of the attack zone, defender can proceed to keep moving away from the attacker.

Caution: Do not move too late!
Caution: Do not move too soon or attacker will have time to adjust (reaction time) and follow/track you.
Caution: Crossing feet up is another common mistake.
Caution: Beware of obstacles in your environment.

Core Energy Principle

Core Energy

Our central and most essential part of our strength and power is our core energy. Without core energy we rely on our extremities which are not as strong as our central core. All defensive tactics techniques utilize this essential principle.

Having Core Energy will:

✓ Give YOU advantage over subjects.

✓ Provide YOU power for counter blocks/defenses.

✓ Help the YOU better control and decentralize a physically resistive subject.

Objective

Demonstrate how to correctly use your core energy.

Performance—Core Energy

1. Partner exercise (A & B)

2. Partner A faces partner B with his/her elbows away from their core.

3. Partner B moves forward toward partner A. Partner A pushes partner B back by pushing at their shoulders. How did it go? Reverse roles.

4. Partner A again, faces partner B with his/her elbows down towards their core.

5. Partner B moves forward toward partner A. Partner A pushes partner B back by pushing at their shoulders. How did it go? Reverse roles.

Defensive Verbalization

During all Defenses: Use loud repetitive Defensive Verbalizations

➡ NO!
➡ STOP!
➡ GET BACK!
➡ STOP RESISTING!
➡ BREAK YOUR FALL!
➡ WERE GOING DOWN ONTO THE GROUND!

Defensive Verbalization:
Creates witnesses
Establishes authority
Keeps YOU breathing
May be used a distraction
Alerts other of a confrontation
Provides direction to the aggressor
Mitigates liability risk to YOU and your agency

The Art of Distraction

Is a process by which we buy valuable time to **Escape, Defend** or **Control.**

Sounds (Loud Scream/Yell) - Movements – Psychological - Lights

Distractions affect the senses which take time for the mind to process the new information. They mainly affect a person's sight and sense of hearing; however, psychological distractions such as asking a person something completely out of the ordinary can cause a mental delay as well. Distractions have been used since ancient times. A valuable advantage!

Sounds: Using a loud scream or yell can cause a momentary delay.

Movements: Using your hands, eyes, and body can distract and cause a momentary delay.

Psychological: Asking a person something completely out of the ordinary can cause them a mental delay.

Lights: Flashlights, the sun, emergency lights, etc., can cause a delay.

Escape Strategies

- Escape is the act or instance of breaking free from danger or threat, or from being trapped, restrained, confined or isolated against your will.

- Planning is the cognitive process of thinking about what you will do in the event of something happening.

Reactionary Gap

The Reactionary Gap is 4-6 Feet. "Action beats Reaction with-in the Reactionary Gap"
The distance between and individual and an agressoe in which the ability to react is impaired due to the close proximity of the agressor.

Hand Positions

There are six basic hand positions.

Objective

Demonstrate how to correctly use your hands in the stop, caution, defensive, authoritative, directive and open positions.

Performance—<u>Stop or Caution</u> Hand Positions

1. Assume the bladed stance
2. Position your arms with your elbows down and you palms facing outward.
3. The non-verbal message says "don't come close to me," or a non-threatening message if you are moving forward

Performance—<u>Defensive or Authoritative</u> Hand Positions

1. Assume the bladed stance
2. Position your arms with your elbows down and your palms in a bladed position.
3. Position your arms with your elbows down and your palms down.
3. The nonverbal message is defensive or authority.

- **Caution:** Closing your hands into a fist position may send a message of aggression.

Performance—<u>Directive or Open</u> Hand Positions

1. Assume the bladed Stance
2. Position your arms and hands pointing with your hand in the direction you want someone to go.
3. Position your arms with your elbows down and your palms facing upward.

- **Caution:** Do not point when giving directions, as pointing is perceived as a derogatory gesture.

Initial Contact Front (1 Person)

Initial Contact (1 person)

Is a technique that teaches individuals how to safely approach a subject and make initial contact.

Objective

Demonstrate how to safely approach a subject while moving forward with defensive movement to make physical contact.

Note: A two person Initial Contact is safer as you have controlled both arms of the aggressor.

Note: This technique can be done to the front or behind the subject. It is safer to perform from behind the subject.

Performance—Initial Contact (1 person)

1. Move forward towards subject at a 45-degree angle.

2. Use defensive movement and keep your hands in the caution position.

3. Your body should be bladed away (vulnerable line) from the subject. Left side forward on left side of subject and right side forward on right side of subject.

4. Firmly capture the elbow of the subject with both hands (thumbs up).

5. Bring your shoulder slightly forward to further protect your vulnerable line if you are in front of the subject. Avoid this if you are behind the subject.

Caution: Armed individuals should keep gun side back and away from the subject regardless of their approaching side.

Caution: Approaching a subject to the front is more dangerous for the individual than approaching from behind.

Initial Contact Front (2 Person)

Initial Contact (2 person)
Is a technique that teaches individuals how to safely approach a subject and make contact.

Objective
Demonstrate how to safely approach a subject while moving forward with defensive movement to make physical contact.

Note: A two person Initial Contact is safer as you have controlled both arms of the aggressor

Note: This technique can be done to the front or behind the subject. It is safer to perform from behind the subject.

Performance—Initial Contact (2 person)

1. Move forward towards subject at a 45-degree angle.
2. Use defensive movement and keep your hands in the caution position.
3. Your body should be bladed away (vulnerable line) from the subject. Left side forward on left of subject and right side forward on right side of subject.
4. Firmly capture the elbow of the subject with both hands (thumbs up).
5. Bring your shoulder slightly forward to further protect your vulnerable line if you are in front of the subject. Avoid this if you are behind the subject.

Caution: Armed individuals should keep gun side back and away from the subject regardless of their approaching side.

Caution: Approaching a subject to the front is more dangerous for the individuals than approaching from behind.

Initial Contact Rear (1 Person)

Initial Contact (1 person)
Is a technique that teaches individuals how to safely approach a subject and make initial contact.

Objective
Demonstrate how to safely approach a subject while moving forward with defensive movement to make physical contact.

Note: A two person Initial Contact is safer as you have controlled both arms of the aggressor.

Note: This technique can be done to the front or behind the subject. It is safer to perform from behind the subject.

Performance—Initial Contact (1 person)

1. Move forward towards subject at a 45-degree angle.

2. Use defensive movement and keep your hands in the caution position.

3. Your body can be (but not necessary) bladed away (vulnerable line) from the subject. Left side forward on left of subject and right side forward on right side of subject.

4. Firmly capture the elbow of the subject with both hands (thumbs up).

Caution: Armed individuals should keep gun side back and away from the subject regardless of their approaching side.

Caution: Approaching a subject to the front is more dangerous for the individual than approaching from behind.

Initial Contact Rear (2 Person)

Initial Contact (2 person)
Is a technique that teaches individuals how to safely approach a subject and make contact.

Objective
Demonstrate how to safely approach a subject while moving forward with defensive movement to make physical contact.

Note: A two person Initial Contact is safer as you have controlled both arms of the aggressor

Note: This technique can be done to the front or behind the subject. It is safer to perform from behind the subject.

Performance—Initial Contact (1 or 2 person)

1. Move forward towards subject at a 45-degree angle.
2. Use defensive movement and keep your hands in the caution position.
3. Your body can be (but not necessary) bladed away (vulnerable line) from the subject. Left side forward on left of subject and right side forward on right side of subject.
4. Firmly capture the elbow of the subject with both hands (thumbs up).

Caution: Armed individuals should keep gun side back and away from the subject regardless of their approaching side.

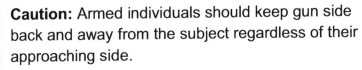

Caution: Approaching a subject to the front is more dangerous for the individuals than approaching from behind.

Contact and Cover Positioning

Contact and Cover (Team Positioning) is the main strategy for AVADE® Defensive Control Tactics. Contact and Cover techniques are used by individuals during situations where they are dealing with a subject(s). The purpose of the technique is to deter a situation from getting out of control and to improve the individual's safety by having other individuals in a constant state of preparation to act in the event that the situation gets out of control.

Contact (Team Leader)

The contact individual is the focal point for the subject as this individual is the primary communicator giving directions to the subject. In many situations the contact individual(s) will initiate communications.

In the pictures the contact individual is communicating with subject which may act as a distraction, allowing cover individuals (team members) to move in and gain physical control if needed. The contact individual should have a prearranged "cue" (verbal or non-verbal) alerting the cover individuals to initiate physical control.

Cover (Team Members)

The cover individual(s) role is to watch subject(s) for any attempt to flee or assault the contact individual. The cover individual(s) should be ever vigilant and ready to respond, and alert the contact individual of suspicious activity or an imminent attempt to assault the contact individual.

Special Note: Cover individuals should maintain their distance (stay back) until needed (see top picture). Moving in too soon may cause subject to feel as though he/she is being corned.

Contact and Cover should be used for all situations involving subjects and witnesses.

Escort Strategies and Techniques (1 Person)

Escort Technique (1 person)
Is a technique that teaches individuals how to safely escort a cooperative subject.

Objective
Demonstrate how to safely escort a cooperative subject using proper distancing, verbal communications and non-verbal communication.

Performance—Escort Technique (1 person)

1. Maintain a 45-degree angle and distance of (4-6 feet) behind the individual.
2. Direct subject where you want them to go
3. Use proper verbal and non-verbal skills.
4. Do not point, use open hand gestures.
5. Maintain Awareness.

Caution: If subject stops and moves towards you, use verbal and non-verbal communication and defensive movements.

Escort Strategies and Techniques (2 Person)

Escort Technique (2 person)
Is a technique that teaches individuals how to safely escort a cooperative subject.

Objective
Demonstrate how to safely escort a cooperative subject using proper distancing, verbal communications and non-verbal communication.

Performance—Escort Technique (2 person)

1. Maintain a 45-degree angle and distance of 4-6 feet behind the individual.
2. Direct subject where you want them to go.
3. Use proper verbal and non-verbal skills.
4. Do not point, use open hand gestures.
5. Maintain Awareness.

Caution: If subject stops and moves towards you, use verbal and non-verbal communication and defensive movements.

Hands-On Escort Technique (1 Person)

Hands-On Escort Technique (1 person)
Is a technique that teaches an individual how to escort a subject using light subject control.

Objective
Demonstrate how to safely escort a passive resistive subject using light subject control with proper hand and body positioning.

Performance—Hands-On Escort (1 person)

1. From the initial contact position.
2. If you are on the right side of the subject your right hand slides down and grips the wrist. Same for left side.
3. Bring the subjects gripped wrist to the side of your body (holstered position).
4. The subjects palm should be facing upward and above any defensive tools you may be carrying.
5. Maintain a 45-degree angle behind the subject and escort them to the desired location.

Caution: When gripping the appropriate wrist, the web of your hand should be on the ulna side of the subject's wrist. This ensures that there core strength is eliminated due to proper positioning.

Caution: When initiating the hands-on escort and when moving the subject, remember to stay at a 45-degree angle behind the subject.

Hands-On Escort Technique (2 Person)

Hands-On Escort Technique (2 person)
Is a technique that teaches individuals how to escort a subject using light subject control.

Objective
Demonstrate how to safely escort a passive resistive subject using light subject control with proper hand and body positioning.

Performance—Hands-On Escort (2 person)

1. From the initial contact position.

2. The individual on the right side of the subject will slide their right hand down and grip the wrist. Same for left side.

3. Bring the subjects gripped wrist to the side of your body (holstered position).

4. The subjects palm should be facing upward and above any defensive tools you may be carrying.

5. Maintain a 45-degree angle behind the subject and escort them to the desired location.

Caution: When gripping the appropriate wrist, the web of your hand should be on the ulna side of the subject's wrist. This ensures that there core strength is eliminated due to proper positioning.

Caution: When initiating the hands-on escort and when moving the subject, remember to stay at a 45-degree angle behind the subject.

Caution: Both individuals acting with the same timing and control can reduce the possibility of escalation.

Control and Decentralization Techniques — One Arm Take-Down

One Arm Take-Down (part 1)
Is a technique that teaches an individual how decentralize a resistive subject using a take-down control technique.

Objective
Demonstrate how to control a subject using a one-bar take-down for a subject who is actively resisting.

Performance—One Arm Take-Down (part 1)

1. From the hands-on escort position.

2. The individual will place their wrist onto the tricep of the subject (2 -3" above the elbow).

3. The individual will then apply pressure to the tricep while moving forward or pivoting to the rear.

4. Use loud defensive verbalizations (NO, STOP, STOP RESISTING, WERE GOING DOWN, BREAK YOUR FALL, to direct the aggressor to stop resisting you and to direct them down.

Caution: Be aware of your environment and what direction you are moving the resistive subject towards.

Control and Decentralization Techniques — One Arm Take-Down (Part 2)

One-Arm Take-Down (part 2)

Is a technique that teaches an individual how decentralize a resistive subject using a take-down control technique.

Objective

Demonstrate how to control a subject using a one-arm take-down for a subject who is actively resisting.

Performance—Arm-Bar Take-Down (part 2)

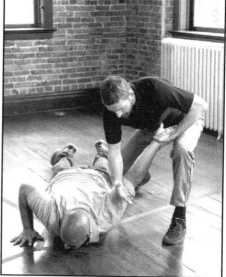

5. Continue to use movement and pressure on the tricep to direct the aggressor to the ground.

6. Use loud defensive verbalizations (NO, STOP, STOP RESISTING, WERE GOING DOWN, BREAK YOUR FALL, to direct the aggressor to stop resisting you and direct them down.

Caution: Be aware of your environment and what direction you are moving the resistive subject towards.

Caution: The prone position is a temporary position which may predispose the subject to breathing difficulties.

Continuously monitor subject and seek medical attention if needed.

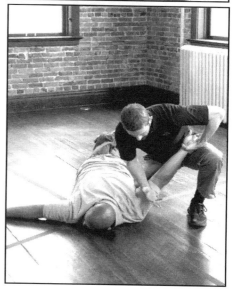

Prone Control Positions

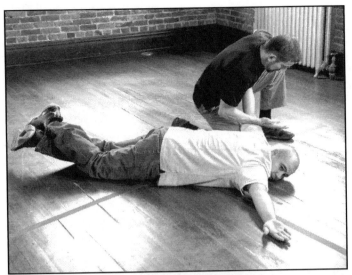

Prone Position Caution

• Individuals in a prone position may have difficulty breathing.

• Monitor individuals and place them on their side, seated position or get them up as soon as possible.

Prone Control is a temporary position!

Positional asphyxia: Positional asphyxia is a form of asphyxia which occurs when someone's position prevents them from breathing adequately. A small but significant number of people die suddenly and without apparent reason during restraint by police, prison (corrections) officers and health care staff. Positional asphyxia may be a factor in some of these deaths.

Research has suggested that restraining a person in a face down position is likely to cause greater restriction of breathing than restraining a person face up.

Many law enforcement and health personnel are now taught to avoid restraining people face down or to do so only for a very short period of time.

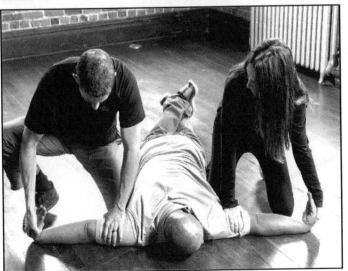

Prone Control is a temporary position!

Standing the Prone Subject

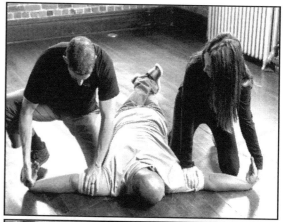

Standing the Prone Subject
Is a technique that teaches an individual(s) how to stand a prone controlled subject.

Objective
Demonstrate how to stand a subject who has been placed in a prone controlled position (one or two individuals are needed).

Performance—Standing the Prone Subject
1. Once control is established verbalize to the subject to place their hands in the push up position.

2. Direct them to push their knees up under them to prepare to stand.

3. Maintain contact with the subject arms and wrists and also prepare to stand up as well.

4. Bring one of the subject's wrists to the holster position on the side of your body.

5. Once control is established by holstering one wrist, the second person will holster the subjects other wrist.

6. Once both wrists are holstered have the subject raise one knee.

7. You will need to have subject raise their torso in order to get them to place one knee if front of them.

8. Ask subject to then stand up completely. Direct the subject where you want them to go.

Caution: Verbalization and constant control is the key to standing a prone controlled subject. Maintain your balance and be prepared to escape if needed.

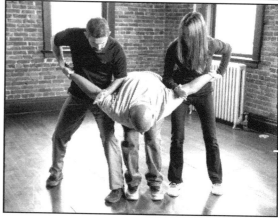

Rear Arm Control Technique

Rear Arm Control Technique (part 1)
Is a technique that teaches an individual how to control a resistive subject from the escort technique.

Objective
Demonstrate how to control a resistive subject using the rear arm control technique from the hands-on escort position.

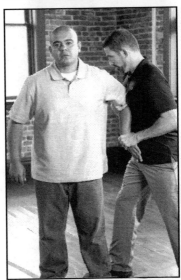

Performance—Rear Arm Control Technique (part 1)

1. From the hands-on escort position.
2. The subject becomes resistive by pushing their arm backward.
3. The individual moves with the resistance and repositions him/herself turning 90 degree towards the aggressor.
4. The individual pulls the resistive subjects arm into his/her core.
5. Use loud defensive verbalizations (NO, STOP, STOP RESISTING, to direct the aggressor to stop resisting you.

Caution: Tuck your head into the shoulder of the aggressor. This will prevent the aggressor from striking you with a rear head butt.

Rear Arm Control Technique (Part 2)

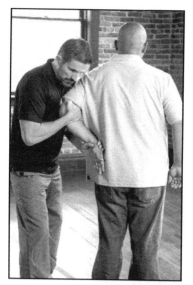

Rear Arm Control Technique (part 2)
Is a technique that teaches an individual how to control a resistive subject from the escort technique.

Objective
Demonstrate how to control a resistive subject using the rear arm control technique from the hands-on escort position.

Performance—Rear Arm Control Technique (part 2)

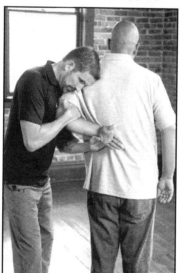

6. Continue to control the arm in your core by pulling it into you.

7. Reposition your hand on the wrist; bring your fingertips onto the resistive subject's knuckles.

8. Gently bring the subject's arm upward into their lower back as you bring the subject's fingertips towards you.

9. Use loud defensive verbalizations (NO, STOP, STOP RESISTING, to direct the aggressor to stop resisting you.

From the rear arm control you can:

- Escort the subject
- Handcuff the subject

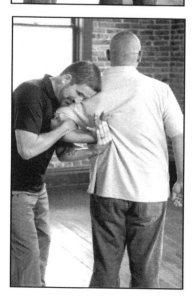

Caution: Tuck your head into the shoulder of the resistive subject. This will prevent the subject from striking you with a rear head butt.

Elements of Reporting Self-Defense or Force

Report and Document: After any situation involving control or defense of yourself or another person, proper documentation and reporting is crucial. The events of the assault or attempted assault should be reported to security/police. The police/security will document the incident and start an investigation. You should also document the account for your own internal records. This can protect you in a possible legal situation that could arise out of using force to defend yourself. As you document your account of the incident make sure to report to security/police any details you missed during your initial report to them.

- **What type of force/self-defense was used during the incident?** Be specific in your documentation regarding the type of control, defense and force that was used during the incident.

- **How long did the incident and resistance last?** Important to note the length of the resistance as this is a factor relative to exhaustion and increasing the level of force.

- **Was any de-escalation used?** Verbal and non-verbal de-escalation techniques should be noted.

- **Were you in fear of injury (bodily harm) to yourself, others or the subject?** Fear is a distressing emotion aroused by perceived threat, impending danger, evil or pain.

- **If so, Why?** Fear is a basic survival mechanism occurring in response to a specific stimulus, such as pain or the threat of danger.

Thoroughly explain, and make sure to document completely.
The importance of documentation cannot be over emphasized. Documentation ensures proper training standards are met, policies and procedures are understood, certification standards are met, liability and risk management mitigation, and departmental and organizational requirements are maintained. A ruling in the United States, Whiteley v. Warden, 410 U.S. 560 (1971), states, that if it is not documented (training and the incident specifics), it did not happen. Therefore, if you do not document your training, a court may rule that training did not occur.

Special Note Every person must take into consideration their moral, legal and ethical beliefs, rights and understandings when using any type of force to defend themselves or others.
Personal Safety Training Inc. makes no legal declaration, representation or claim as to what force should be used or not used during a self-defense/assault incident or situation. Each trainee must take into consideration their ability, agency policies and procedures and state and federal laws.

Levels of Force & Defense

The following chart is designed to give you a basic understanding of how your actions may apply to the actions of an aggressive subject. Your action may need to increase or decrease dependent upon the situation. Any Use-of-Force or Self-Defense MUST be lawful.

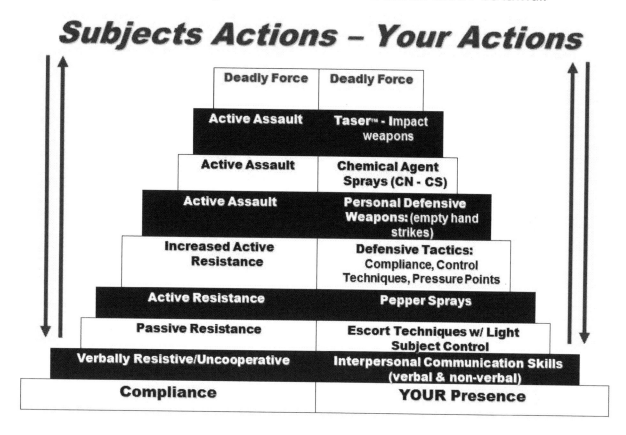

Lawful Use-of-Force & Defense is permissible:

5. When used to control an out of control individual
6. When used to overcome resistance of the out of control individual
7. When used to prevent escape from an individual who is under your control (hold)
8. When used in self-defense or in the defense of others

Use of Force & Self-Defense <u>MUST</u> be Reasonable
YOU should always take into consideration the <u>facts</u> and the <u>circumstances</u> of the incident.

➡ Type of crime and severity of the crime

➡ Resistance of the subject when needing to control them

➡ The threat and safety to others in the area

➡ Aggressive Subject and Staff Factors

Aggressive Subject and Staff Factors

Many factors may affect your selection of an appropriate level of use-of-force or self-defense. These factors should be articulated in your post incident documentation.

Examples may include:

Age: In dealing with an aggressive subject who is agile, younger, faster, stronger, and has more stamina an older staff person may have to use more force/control/defense. In contrast a younger staff person would use less control/force/defense on an older person.

Size: In dealing with a larger aggressive subject, a smaller staff person may need to use more force/control/defense during the incident. A larger staff person would obviously, use less force/control/defense an aggressive subject who is smaller.

Skill Level: In dealing with a subject who is skilled in mixed martial arts or an expert in karate, it may be more difficult to control or defend against them based on their skill level. A staff person who is skilled in defensive tactics, may only need to use a minimum of force (with proper technique) to control/defend the subject. A staff person without current training and experience may need to use more force/defense to control or defend against the subject.

Relative Strength: The different body composition of males and females may be a factor in controlling a member of the opposite gender. Females typically have less torso strength than their male counterparts. A male staff may have to use less force to control a female subject. Whereas, a female staff person may need to use more force to control a male subject.

Multiple Aggressors: A staff person who is being physically attacked by multiple aggressors is at a disadvantage. Even a highly skilled staff involved in defensive tactics is likely to be harmed in a situation such as this. In order to survive multiple aggressor attacks, higher levels of force may be necessary.

Special Note:
Every person must take into consideration their moral, legal, and ethical beliefs and rights and understandings when using any type of force to defend themselves or others. Personal Safety Training Inc. makes no legal declaration, representation or claim as to what force should be used or not used during a self-defense/assault incident or situation. Each individual must take into consideration their ability, agency policies and procedures and laws in their state and/or country.

AVADE® Healthcare Restraint Holds/Applications

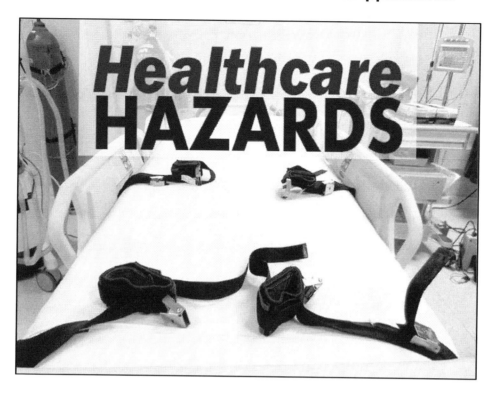

- Using restraints to control violence is acceptable in certain cases, but clinical policy and procedures must be rigidly adhered to.

- Restraint use is very controversial and not always understood by staff. Acceptability of restraint use should be carefully identified and approved by medical staff.

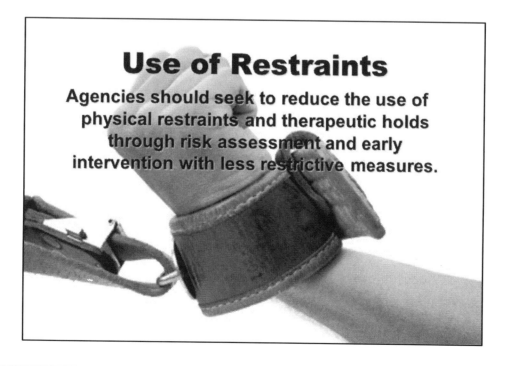

Supine Healthcare Restraint

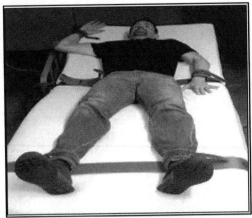

Supine Healthcare Restraint
The following pictures depict a 4pt healthcare restraint for a behavioral/violent person restraint application.

Objective
Demonstrate how to hold and apply healthcare restraints to a combative/violent individual.

Performance—Supine Restraint Hold/Application

1. Once staff (2 persons) have placed an individual on the bed they (+ 2 other staff) will hold them down on either side of the elbow and knee. Not on joint!
2. A 5th staff person can then apply restraints to the ankles and wrists.
3. By keeping one arm raised above head, it reduces the individual's ability to use their core strength and resist.
4. A 6th person may be needed to control the individuals head.
5. A 7th staff person may be needed to control the individual's feet until restraints can be applied.

Note: Restraints can be removed for a 3pt, 2pt or even 1pt restraint. Follow your SOP's.

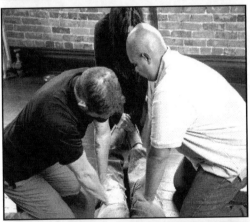

During all Defenses:
- Use loud repetitive defensive verbalizations (NO, STOP, STOP RESISTING, etc…) to direct the aggressor to stop resisting you.

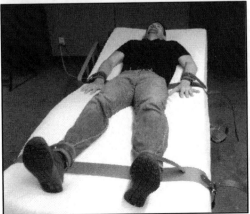

Always:
- Follow agency policies and procedures in regard to restraint and seclusion.
- Report and Document immediately.

Risk Factors for Restraints

Risk Factors for Restraints:

➡ Patients who smoke

➡ Positional Asphyxiation

➡ Patients with deformities

➡ Improper restraining Techniques

➡ Incomplete medical assessment

➡ Improper restraints, room and beds

➡ Insufficient staff orientation and training

➡ Supine position may predispose them to aspiration

➡ Prone may predispose them to suffocation

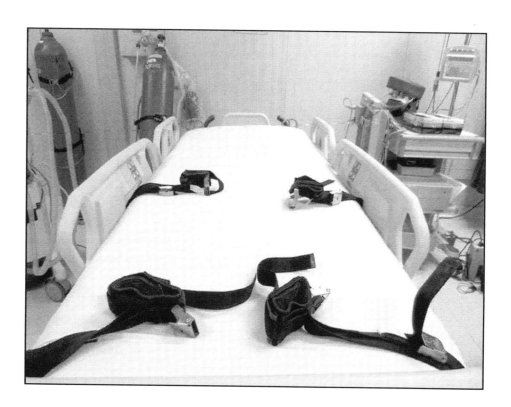

Strategies for Reducing Risk

➢ Reduce use of physical restraints and holds through risk assessments and early interventions.

➢ Clarification of restraint use in clinical protocols.

➢ See alternatives to restraint use (de-escalation techniques).

➢ Enhance staff orientation/education regarding alternatives and proper application.

➢ Develop structured procedures / competency for consistent application of restraints.

➢ Develop safety guidelines and continuous observation of those restrained.

➢ The "one-hour" rule.

➢ Utilize patient quiet rooms/seclusion rooms.

➢ Revise the staffing model.

➢ Increase awareness of medical/surgical vs. behavioral restraints.

➢ Comply to JCAHO and State/Federal Standards

Strategies for Reducing Risk (Part 2)

➢ If patient is restrained in the supine position, ensure that head is free to rotate and when possible, the head of the bed is elevated to minimize the risk of aspiration.

➢ If patient must be controlled in the prone position, ensure that airway is unobstructed at all times (do not cover or bury the patients face). Ensure that patient can expand their lungs to properly breathe (do not put any pressure on their back).

  • Special caution is required for children, elderly patients and very obese patients.

➢ Never place a towel, bag or other cover over a patients face.

➢ Do not restrain a patient in a bed with unprotected split side rails.

➢ Do not use certain types of restraints, such as high vests and waist restraints.

➢ Ensure patient is properly searched and free of weapons and smoking materials.

  • This would also include limiting access from friends and family

**Policy and Procedures should be adhered to for all
Healthcare Restraint Applications/Holds**

Chemical Restraints

A **chemical restraint** is a form of medical restraint in which a drug is used to restrict the freedom or movement of a patient, or in some cases, to sedate a patient. These are used in emergency, acute, and psychiatric settings to control aggressive patients who are interfering with their care or who are otherwise harmful to themselves or others.

Drugs that are often used as chemical restraints include benzodiazepines (such as Lorazepam (Ativan), Midazolam (Versed), or Diazepam (Valium). Haloperidol (Haldol) is a drug chemically unrelated to benzodiazepines and is also popular for chemical restraint, without the potentially dangerous side effects of benzodiazepine drugs.

Any use of chemical restraints must be authorized and administered by a licensed clinician or doctor.

Positional Asphyxia

Positional asphyxia is a form of asphyxia which occurs when someone's position prevents them from breathing adequately. A small but significant number of people die suddenly and without apparent reason during restraint by police, prison (corrections) officers and health care staff. Positional asphyxia may be a factor in some of these deaths.

- Positional asphyxia is a potential danger of some physical restraint techniques.
- People may die from positional asphyxia by simply getting themselves into a breathing-restricted position they cannot get out of, either through carelessness or as a consequence of another accident.

Research has suggested that restraining a person in a face down position is likely to cause greater restriction of breathing than restraining a person face up. Many law enforcement and health personnel are now taught to avoid restraining people face down or to do so only for a very short period of time.

Risk factors which may increase the chance of death include: Obesity, Prior Cardiac or Respiratory Problems, Alcohol Intoxication, Illicit drugs such as cocaine and Excited Delirium "Bizarre or Frenzied Behavior" (mental disease including psychosis and schizophrenia and/or drug intoxication).

Excited Delirium

Excited delirium is a controversial term used to explain deaths of individuals in police custody, in which the person being arrested or restrained shows some combination of agitation, violent or bizarre behavior, insensitivity to pain, elevated body temperature, or increased strength. It has been listed as a cause of death by some medical examiners.

- The term has no formal medical recognition and is not recognized in the Diagnostic and Statistical Manual of Mental Disorders. There may also be a controversial link between "excited delirium" deaths and the use of Tasers to subdue agitated people.

- Almost all subjects who have died during restraint have engaged in extreme levels of physical resistance against the restraint for a prolonged period of time.

- Other issues in the way the subject is restrained can also increase the risk of death; for example, kneeling or otherwise placing weight on the subject and particularly any type of restraint hold around the subject's neck.

About the Author

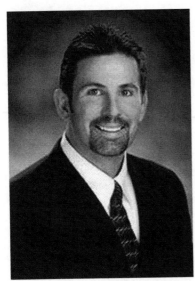

David Fowler is the founder and president of (PSTI) Personal Safety Training Incorporated and AVADE Training, located in Coeur d' Alene, ID. He is responsible for the overall management and operations of PSTI and AVADE, which offers seminars, training, consulting, and protective details. Since 1990, David has been involved security operations, training, and protective details.

He is the author of the SOCS® (Security Oriented Customer Service) program and training manual as well as the AVADE® Personal Safety Training and Workplace Violence Prevention programs and training manuals. He is also the author of book *Be Safe Not Sorry - The art and science of keeping YOU and your family safe from crime and violence*. David has worked with thousands of individuals and hundreds of agencies and corporations throughout the United States and Canada. His presentations have included international, national and local seminars. David's thorough understanding of safety and security, and martial science add an exciting and interesting approach to his style of presentation.

David is a certified master instructor in several nationally recognized training programs such as Workplace Violence Prevention (AVADE®), Pepper Spray Defense™, Handcuffing Tactics™, Security Oriented Customer Service (SOCS®), Defensive Tactics System™ (DTS™), Defense Baton™, Security Incident Reporting System™ (SIRS™) and AVADE® Personal Safety Training. David has certified and trained thousands of individuals in these programs and others throughout the United States and abroad.

He is a Graduate of (ESI) Executive Security International's advanced Executive Protection Program and the Protective Intelligence and Investigations program. A member of ASIS (American Society for Industrial Security), The International Law Enforcement Educators & Trainers Association (ILEETA) and the International Association of Healthcare Safety & Security (IAHSS).

David brings insight, experience, and a passion for empowering people and organizations utilizing the training programs and protective services that he offers here in the United States and in other countries. He is considered by many to be the most dynamic and motivational speaker and trainer in the security and personal safety industry.

David is happily married to the love of his life, Genelle Fowler. They live in Coeur d' Alene, ID and have five children and one grandchild. David and Genelle have committed their lives to serving others through the mission of safety. Both David and Genelle travel extensively, providing training and consulting to corporations throughout North America.

Bibliography, Reference Guide and Recommended Reading

Books, CD's, DVD's and Websites

Adams, Terry and Rob. *Seminar Production Business: Your Step by Step Guide to Success.* Entrepreneur Press, Canada 2003.

Albrect, Steve. *Surviving Street Patrol: The Officer's Guide to Safe and Effective Policing.* Paladin Press, Boulder, CO 2001.

Amdur, Ellis. *Dueling with O-sensei: Grappling with the Myth of the Warrior Sage.* Edgework, Seattle, WA 2000.

Andersen, Peter A. *The Complete Idiot's Guide to Body Language.* Alpha Books, Indianapolis, IN 2004.

Andrews, Andy. *The Travelers Gift: Seven Decisions that Determine Personal Success.* Nelsen Books, Nashville Tennessee, 2002.

Arapakis, Maria. *Soft Power: How to Speak Up, Set Limits, and Say No Without Losing Your Lover, Your Job, or Your Friends.* Warner Books Inc. NY, NY 1990.

Artwhohl, Alexis & Christensen, Loren. *Deadly Force Encounters: What Cops need to know to mentally and physically prepare for and survive a gunfight.* Paladin Press, Boulder, CO 1997.

ASIS International. *Security Management Magazine.* www.securitymanagment.com 2006-2016.

Brown, Tom. *Survival Guides: Americas Bestselling Wilderness Series.* Berkley Books, New York, 1984.

Byrnes, John D. *Before Conflict: Preventing Aggressive Behavior.* Scarecrow Press, Lanham, Maryland and Oxford 2002.

Canfield, Jack and Switzer, Janet. *The Success Principles: How to Get from Where You Are to Where You Want to Be.* Harper Collins Publishers, NY, NY 2005.

Canfield, Jack and Bunch, Jim. *The Ultimate Life Workshop: 7 Strategies for Creating the Ultimate Life.* Live Workshop - February 2008.

Carnegie, Dale. *Golden Book.* www.dalecarnegie.com

Carnegie, Dale. *How to Win Friends & Influence People*. Pocket Books, NY, NY 1936.

Chodron, Thubten. *Working With Anger*. Snow Lion Publication, Ithaca, NY 2001.

Christenson, Loren. *DEFENSIVE TACTICS: Modern Arrest & Control Techniques for Today's Police Warrior*. Turtle Press, Washington, DC 2008

Christenson, Loren. *Fighting in the Clinch: Vicious Strikes, Street Wrestling, and Gouges for Real Fights*. Paladin Press, Boulder, CO 2009

Christensen, Loren. *The Way Alone: Your Path to Excellence in the Martial Arts*. Paladin Press, Boulder, CO 1987.

Christensen, Loren. *Warriors: On Living with Courage, Discipline and Honor*. Paladin Press, Boulder, CO 2004.

Covey, Stephen R. *The 7 Habits of Highly Effective People: Powerful Lessons in Personal Change*. Fireside, NY, NY 1989.

Covey, Stephen R. *The 8th Habit: From Effectiveness to Greatness*. Better Life Media, DVD and CD, 2004.

Day Laura, *Practical Intuition*. Villard Books, NY, NY 1996

DeBecker, Gavin. *The Gift of Fear*. Dell Publishing, NY, NY 1997.

DeBecker, Gavin. *Fear Less: Real Truth about Risk, Safety, and Security in a Time of Terrorism*. Little Brown and Company, Boston, NY, London 2002.

DeBecker, Gavin & Taylor, Tom & Marquart, Jeff. *Just 2 Seconds: Using Time and Space to Defeat Assassins*. The Gavin DeBecker Center for the Study and Reduction of Violence a not-for-profit foundation, Studio City, CA 2008.

DeBecker, Gavin. *Protecting the Gift: Keeping Children and Teenagers Safe (and Parents Sane)*. A Dell Trade Paperback, NY, NY 1999.

Deshimaru, Taisen. *The Zen Way to the Martial Arts: A Japanese Master Reveals the Secrets of the Samurai*. Penguin Compass. NY, NY 1982.

DeMasco, Steve. *The Shaolin Way: 10 Modern Secrets of Survival from a Shaolin Kung Fu Grandmaster*. Harper, NY, NY 2006.

Divine, Mark. *The WAY of the SEAL: Think Like an Elite Warrior to Lead and Succeed.* Readers Digest, White Plains, NY 2013

Dyer, Wayne. *The Power of Intention; Learning to Co-Create your world your way.* Hay House, CA 2004.

Eckman, Paul. *Emotions Revealed: Recognizing Faces and Feelings to Improve Communication and Emotional Life.* Henry Holt & Company, NY, NY 2007.

Eckman, Paul. *Telling Lies.* WW. Norton Company, NY and London. 1991.

Eggerichs, Emerson. *Love & Respect: The Love She Most Desires and The respect he Desperately Needs.* Gale Cengage Learning. US 2010

Fowler, David. *Be Safe Not Sorry, the Art and Science of keeping YOU and your family Safe from Crime and Violence.* Personal Safety Training Inc. Coeur d Alene, ID 2011.

Fowler, David. *Violence In The Workplace: Education, Prevention & Mitigation.* Personal Safety Training Inc. Coeur d Alene, ID 2012.

Fower, David. *To Serve and Protect: Providing SERVICE while maintaining SAFETY in the Workplace.* Personal Safety Training Inc. Coeur d Alene, ID 2015

Funakoshi, Gichen. *Karate-Do My Way of Life.* Kodansha International, Tokyo, NY. London, 1975.

Gallo, Carmine. *Inspire Your Audience: 7 Keys to Influential Presentations.* Paper. Communication Skills Coach – Author of Fire Them Up!

Gardner, Daniel. *The Science of Fear: How the Culture of Fear MANIPULATES YOUR BRAIN.* Penguin Books Ltd, Strand, London 2009

Garner, Bryan. *Black's Law Dictionary: Seventh Edition.* West Group, St. Paul, MN, 1999.

Gawain, Shakti. *Creative Visualization.* New World Library, Novato, CA 2002.

Gawain, Shakti. *Developing Intuition: Practical Guide for Daily Life.* New World Library, Novato, CA 2000.

Gilligan, James. *VIOLENCE: Reflections on a National Epidemic.* Vintage Books, NY 1996

Gladwell, Malcolm. *Blink.* Little, Brown & Company, NY 2005.

Glennon, Jim. *Arresting Communication: Essential Interaction Skills for Law Enforcement.* LifeLine Training & Caliber Press, Elmhurst, IL 2010.

Goleman, Daniel. *Emotional Intelligence.* Bantom Books, NY, NY 2005.

Gray, John. *Beyond Mars and Venus.* Better Life Media, DVD and CD, 2004.

Gregory, Hamilton. *Public Speaking for College and Career: Fifth Edition.* McGraw-Hill, Boston 1999.

Gross, Linden. *Surviving A Stalker: Everything you need to know to keep yourself safe.* Marlowe and Company, NY, NY 2000.

Grossman, Dave & Christensen, Loren. *On Combat: The Psychology of Deadly Conflict in War and Peace.* PPCT Research, IL 2004.

Grossman, Dave & DeGaetano, Gloria. *Stop Teaching our Kids to Kill: A call to action against TV, Movie & Video Game Violence.* Crown Publishers, NY, NY 1999.

Harrell, Keith. *Attitude is Everything: 10 Life Changing Steps to Turning Attitude Into Action.* Harper Collins Publishing, NY, NY 1999.

Hawkins, David R, MD. *Power vs. Force: The Hidden Determinants of Human Behavior.* Veritas, Sedona, AZ 2004.

Headley, Steve. *Assault Prevention Workshop.* Assault Prevention Workshops, LLC 2009.

Hyams, Joe. *Zen in the Martial Arts.* Bantam Books, Toronto, NY, London, Sydney, Auckland, 1982.

IAHSS. *Basic Training Manual and Study Guide for Healthcare Security Officers.* Lombard, IL 1995.

IAHSS. *Journal of Healthcare Protection Management.* Bayside, NY 2008-2016.

Jo-Ellan Dimitrius, Ph.D., and Mark Mazzarella. *Reading People: How to Understand people and Predict their Behavior-Anytime, Anyplace.* Ballantine Books, NY, NY 1999.

Kane, Lawrence A. *Surviving Armed Assaults.* YMAA Publication Center, Boston MA 2006.

Kinnaird, Brian. *Use of Force: Expert Guidance for Decisive Force Response*. Looseleaf Law Publications, Flushing, NY 2003.

Krebs & Henry & Gabriele. *When Violence Erupts: A Survival Guide for Emergency Responders*. The C.V. Mosby Company, St. Louis, Baltimore, Philadelphia, Toronto, 1990.

Larkin, Tim and Ranck-Buhr, Chris. *How to Survive The Most Critical 5 Seconds of Your Life*. The TFT Group. Sequim, WA 2008

Lawler, Jennifer. *Dojo Wisdom: 100 Simple Ways to Become a Stronger, Calmer, more Courageous Person*. Penguin Compass, NY, NY 2003.

Leaf, Caroline. *Switch on your Brain: The key to Peak Happiness, Thinking, and Health*. Baker Books, Grand Rapids, MI 2013

Lee, Bruce. *Tao of Jeet Kune Do*. Ohara Publications, Santa Clarita, CA 1975.

Lee, Johnny. *Addressing Domestic Violence in the Workplace*. HRD Press, Inc. Amherst, MA 2005

Lee, Linda. *The Bruce Lee Story*. Ohara Publications, Santa Clarita, CA 1989.

Lion, John, MD. *Evaluation and Management of the Violent Patient: Guidelines in the Hospital and Institution*. Charles C. Thomas Publisher, Springfield, IL 1972.

Little, John. *The Warrior Within: The philosophies of Bruce Lee to better understand the world around you and achieve a rewarding life*. Contemporary Books, Chicago, IL 1996.

Loehr, James and Migdwo, Jeffrey. Breathe In Breathe Out: Inhale Energy and Exhale Stress By Guiding and Controlling Your Breathing. Time Life Books, Alexandria, VI 1986

Lorenz, Conrad. *On Aggression*. MJF Book. NY1963

Machowicz, Richard J. *Unleash The Warrior Within: Develop the Focus, Discipline, Confidence and Courage You Need to Achieve Unlimited Goals*. Marlowe & Company, NY 2002.

Mackay, Harvey. "Harvey Mackay's Column This Week." Weekly e-mail publication, www.harveymackay.com

MacYoung, Marc "Animal." *Ending Violence Quickly: How Bouncers, Bodyguards and Other Security Professionals Handle Ugly Situations*. Paladin Press, Boulder, CO 1993.

Maggio, Rosalie. *How to Say It: Choice Words, Phrases, Sentences, and Paragraphs for Every Situation*. Prentice Hall Press, NY, NY 2001.

Maltz, Maxwell MD. *Psycho-Cybernetics: A New Way to Get More Living Out Of Life*. Essandress, NY, NY 1960.

Marcinko, Richard. *The Rogue Warriors Strategy For Success*. Pocket Books, NY, NY 1997.

Mason, Tom & Chandley Mark. *Managing Violence and Aggression: A Manual for Nurses and Health Care Workers*. Churchill Livingstone, Edinburgh, 1999.

McGrew, James. *Think Safe: Practical Measures to Increase Security at Home, at Work, and Throughout Life*. Cameo Publications, Hilton Head Island, SC, 2004.

McTaggart, Lynne. *The Intention Experiment: Using Your thoughts to Change Your Life and the World*. Free Press, NY, NY 2007.

Medina, John. *Brain Rules: 12 Principles for Surviving and Thriving at Work, Home, and School*. Pear Press, Seattle, WA 2008.

Miller, Rory. *FACING VIOLENCE: Preparing for the Unexpected-Ethically, Emotionally, Physically, Without Going to Prison*. YMAA Publication Center, Wolfeboro, NH 2011

Murphy, Joseph, Dr. *The Power of Your Subconscious Mind*. Bantam Books, NY, Toronto, London, Sidney, Auckland 2000.

Musashi, Miyamoto. Translated by Thomas Cleary. *The Book of Five Rings*. Shambala, Boston and London 2003.

Norris, Chuck. *The Secret Power Within: Zen Solutions to Real Problems*. Broadway Books, NY 1996.

Norris, Chuck. Winning Tournament Karate. Ohara Publications, Burbank, CA 1975.

Nowicki, Ed. *Total Survival*. Performance Dimensions, Powers Lake, MI 1993.

Omartian, Stormie. *PRAYER WARIOR: The Power of Praying Your Wat to Victory*. Harvest House Publishers, Eugene, OR 2013

Ouellette, Roland W. *Management of Aggressive Behavior*. Performance Dimension Publishing, Powers Lake, WI 1993.

Palumbo, Dennis. *The Secrets of Hakkoryu Jujutsu: Shodan Tactics*. Paladin Press Boulder, CO 1987.

Parker, S.L. *212 the extra degree*. The Walk the Talk Co. 2005 www.walkthetalk.com.

Patire, Tom. *Tom Patire's Personal Protection Handbook*. Three Rivers Press, NY 2003.

Peale, Norman Vincent. *Six Attitudes for Winners*. Tyndale House Publishers, Inc. Wheaton, Il 1989.

Peale, Norman Vincent. *The Power of Positive Thinking*. Ballantine Books, NY, NY 1956.

Pease, Allan and Barbara. *The Definitive Book of Body Language*. Bantam Dell. NY, NY 2004.

Perkins, John & Ridenhour, Al & Kovsky Matt. *Attack Proof: The Ultimate Guide to Personal Protection*. Human Kinetics, Champaign, IL 2000.

Pietsch, William. *HUMAN BE-ING: How to have a creative relationship instead of a power struggle*. Lawrence Hill & Company Publishers Inc, NY, NY 1974

PPCT Management Systems, Inc. *Defensive Tactics Instructor Manual*. PPCT 2005.

Purpura, Philip. *The Security Handbook: Second Edition*. Butterworth Heinemann, Boston, 2003.

Rail, Robert R. *The Unspoken Dialogue: Understanding Body Language and Controlling Interviews and Negotiations*. Varro Press, Kansas City 2001.

Ralston, Peter. *Cheng Hsin: The Principles of Effortless Power*. North Atlantic Books, Berkeley, CA 1989.

Ratey, John J. *Spark: The Revolutionary New Science of Exercise and the Brain*. Little, Brown and Co., NY, NY 2008.

Rawls, Neal. *BE ALERT BE AWARE HAVE A PLAN: The complete guide to protecting yourself, your home, your family*. Globe Pequot Press, Guilford, CT

Rodale Inc. *Men's Health Today 2007*. Rodale Inc. US 2007.

Sandford, John and Paula. *The Transformation of the Inner Man*. Bridge Publishing Inc. S. Plainfield, NJ 1982

Strong, Sanford. *Strong on Defense: Survival Rules to Protect You and Your Family from Crime.* Pocket Books, NY, NY 1996.

Sjodin, Terri. New Sales Speak: *The 9 Biggest Sales Presentation Mistakes and How to Avoid Them.* Better Life Media. DVD and CD 2004.

Soo, Chee, *The Chinese Art of T'ai Chi Ch'uan: The Taoist way to mental and physical health.* The Aquarian Press, Wellingborough, Northamptonshire 1984.

Staley, Charles. *The Science of Martial Arts Training.* Multi Media Books, Burbank, CA 1999.

The Evidence Bible, NKJV, Bridge-Logos Publishers- © 2011 by Ray Comfort. Alachua, FL.

The Results Driven Manager. *Dealing with Difficult People.* Harvard Business School Publishing Corp, Boston MA 2005.

Theriault, Jean Yves. *Full Contact Karate.* Contemporary Books Inc. Chicago, 1983.

The World's Greatest Treasury of Health Secrets. Bottom Line Publications, Stamford, CT 2006.

Thompson, George. *Verbal Judo.* Quill William Morrow, NY 1993.

Tsunetomo, Yamamoto. *Hagakure: The Book of the Samurai.* Kodansha International, Tokyo, NY, London 1979.

Turner, James T. *Violence in the Medical Care Setting.* Aspen Systems Corporation, Rockville, MD 1984.

Tzu, Sun. *The Art of War.* Samuel Griffith Interpretation, Oxford University Press, 1993.

Ueshiba, Kisshomaru. *The Spirit of Aikido.* Kodansha International, Tokyo, NY, London, 1987.

Van Horne, Patrick and Riley, Jason. *LEFT of BANG: How the Marine Corps' Combat Hunter Program Can Save Your Life.* Black Irish Entertainment LLC, NY and Los Angeles, 2014

US Dept. of Justice. *Workplace Violence: Issues in Response.* Critical Incident Response Group, National Center for the Analysis of Violent Crime, FBI Academy, Quantico, Virginia 2001.

Wallace, Bill. *The Ultimate Kick: The Wallace Method to Winning Karate.* Unique Publications, Burbank, CA 1987.

Webster, Noah. *Webster's Dictionary.* Modern Promotions/Publishers, NY, NY 1984.
Willis, Brian. *W.I.N. 2: Insights Into Training and Leading Warriors.* Warrior Spirit Books, Calgary, Alberta, Canada 2009.

Websites and Web links

http://www.AVADEtraining.com

http://www.personalsafetytraining.com

http://www.socstraining.com

http://www.tribalsecuritytraining.com

http://www.wpvprevention.com

http://www.aaets.org/article54.htm

http://en.wikipedia.org/wiki/Excited_delirium

http://en.wikipedia.org/wiki/Chemical_restraint

http://en.wikipedia.org/wiki/Positional_asphyxia

http://www.aele.org/law/2008ALL12/chicago.pdf

http://www.hospitalmedicine.org/AM/Template.cfm?Section=Reference_Material&Template=/CM/ContentDisplay.cfm&ContentID=17070

Workplace Violence: http://cms.nursingworld.org/workplaceviolence

http://helpguide.org/mental/eq4_emotion_communicates.htm

http://hawaii.gov/ag/cpja/quicklinks/workplace_violence/WVfull.pdf

http://www.ena.org/media/PressReleases/Pages/WorkPlaceViolence.aspx

http://www.jointcommission.org/SentinelEvents/SentinelEventAlert/sea_40.htm

http://www.dli.mn.gov/Wsc/PDF/WorkplaceViolencePreventionGuide.pdf

http://www.cbs.state.or.us/external/osha/pdf/workshops/702w.pdf

http://blog.awareity.com/2010/03/04/identifying-red-flags-warning-signs-and-indicators/

http://www.co.midland.tx.us/edp/pdf_files/Misc/Workplace%20-%20Violence.pdf

http://sk.sagepub.com/reference/crimepunishment/n419.xml

http://www.cdc.gov/violenceprevention/pdf/nisvs-fact-sheet-2014.pdf

http://changingminds.org/techniques/body/parts_body_language/eyes_body_language.htm

http://www.phoenixhouse.org/prevention/signs-and-symptoms-of-substance-abuse/

A Circle of Distortion: The Social Construction of Mass Murder in the United States by Grant Duwe. http://wcr.sonoma.edu/v6n1/manuscripts/duwe.pdf

Active Shooter: How To Respond. http://www.alerts.si.edu/docs/DHS_ActiveShooterBook.pdf

Active Shooter: Recommendations and Analysis for Risk Mitigation. http://www.nypdshield.org/public/SiteFiles/documents/ActiveShooter.pdf

ASIS International Active Shooter resource page. http://www.asisonline.org/education/activeShooter.xml

ASIS/SHRM Workplace Violence Prevention and Intervention Standard. http://www.abdi-secure-ecommerce.com/asis/ps-1092-30-1967.aspx

Current Intelligence Bulletin #57: Violence in the Workplace: Risk Factors and Prevention Strategies. http://www.cdc.gov/niosh/docs/96-100/

Effectiveness of Crime Prevention Through Environmental Design (CPTED) in Reducing Robberies, by Carri Casteel, MPH, Corinne Peek-Asa, PhD. http://www.usak.org.tr/istanbul/files/cr.pr.environmental.design.pdf

Effectiveness of Safety Measures Recommended for Prevention of Workplace Homicide, by Dana Loomis, PhD; Stephen W. Marshall, PhD; Susanne H. Wolf, RN, MPH; Carol W. Runyan, PhD; John D. Butts, M.D. http://jama.jamanetwork.com/article.aspx?articleid=194680

Enforcement Procedures for Investigating or Inspecting Workplace Violence Incidents CPL 02-01-052. http://www.osha.gov/OshDoc/Directive_pdf/CPL_02-01-052.pdf

Fatal occupational injuries by industry and event or exposure, All United States, 2009. http://www.bls.gov/iif/oshwc/cfoi/cftb0241.pdf

FEMA EMI IS-907 - Active Shooter: What You Can Do. http://training.fema.gov/EMIWeb/IS/is907.asp

Guidelines for Preventing Workplace Violence for Health Care & Social Service Workers. http://www.osha.gov/Publications/osha3148.pdf

Number and percent distribution of nonfatal occupational injuries and illnesses involving days away from work by event or exposure leading to injury or illness and number of days away from work, private industry, 2009. http://www.bls.gov/iif/oshwc/osh/case/ostb2516.pdfhttp://www.bls.gov/iif/oshwc/osh/case/ostb2516.pdf

Occupational homicides by selected characteristics, 1997-2010. http://www.bls.gov/iif/oshwc/cfoi/work_hom.pdf

Occupational Suicides: Census of Fatal Occupational Injuries Fact Sheet, August 2009. http://bls.gov/iif/oshwc/cfoi/osar0010.pdf

OSHA Workplace Violence. http://www.osha.gov/SLTC/workplaceviolence/

Recommendations for Workplace Violence Prevention Programs in Late-Night Retail Establishments - OSHA Publication 3153. http://www.osha.gov/Publications/osha3153.pdf

Revisions to the 2009 Census of Fatal Occupational Injuries (CFOI) counts. http://www.bls.gov/iif/oshwc/cfoi/cfoi_revised09.pdf

Summary of Research on Mass Murder by John Klofas. http://www.rit.edu/cla/cpsi/WorkingPapers/2009/2009-11.pdf

Ten Tips to Mitigate Workplace Violence and Threats, by Felix P. Nater http://www.securitymagazine.com/articles/83329-10-tips-to-mitigate-workplace-violence-and-threats

The Psychology of Security, by Bruce Schneier. http://www.schneier.com/essay-155.html

The Workplace Violence Prevention eReport.
http://www.workplaceviolence911.com/preventionreport

U.S. BLS Census of Fatal Occupational Injuries (CFOI) 2009 Chart Pack.
http://www.bls.gov/iif/oshwc/cfoi/cfch0008.pdf

U.S. BLS Fatal occupational injuries by selected characteristics: State of incident, employee status, sex, age, race, event or exposure, source, secondary source, nature, part of body, worker activity, location, occupation, and industry, 1992-2002 (revised final counts).
http://www.bls.gov/iif/oshwc/cfoi/cftb0186.pdf

U.S. BLS Table 4, Number, incidence rate, and median days away from work for nonfatal occupational injuries and illnesses involving days away from work by selected detailed occupation and private industry, state government, and local government, 2010.
http://www.bls.gov/news.release/osh2.t04.htm

Violence in the Workplace by Tanya Restrepo and Harry Shuford.
https://www.ncci.com/documents/Workplace_Research.pdf

When Prevention Fails: Minimizing the Post-Incident Impact of Workplace Violence.
http://www.businessinsurance.com/section/NEWS050106

Workplace violence intervention effectiveness: A systematic literature review, by James T. Wassell. http://www.sciencedirect.com/science/article/pii/S092575350800218X

Workplace Violence Prevention: Readiness and Response, by Stephen J. Romano, Micòl E. Levi-Minzi, Eugene A. Rugala, and Vincent B. Van Hasselt.
http://www.fbi.gov/stats-services/publications/law-enforcementbulletin/january2011/workplace_violence_prevention

Workplace Violence, 1993-2009 National Crime Victimization Survey and the Census of Fatal Occupational Injuries.
http://bjs.ojp.usdoj.gov/content/pub/pdf/wv09.pdf

Workplace Violence: Issues in Response, Edited by Eugene A. Rugala and Arnold R. Isaacs.
http://www.fbi.gov/stats-services/publications/workplace-violence

Work-related Homicides: The Facts by Eric Sygnatur and Guy Toscano.
http://www.bls.gov/opub/cwc/archive/spring2000art1.pdf

Work-related multiple-fatality incidents, by Dino Drudi and Mark Zak.
http://www.bls.gov/mlr/2004/10/art2full.pdf

TRAINING COURSES FOR YOU AND YOUR AGENCY

The only way to deal with conflict and avoid violence of any type is through awareness, vigilance, avoidance, defensive training and escape planning."

David Fowler, President of PSTI specializes in nationally recognized training programs which empower individuals, increase confidence and promote pro-active preventative solutions.

OSHA, Labor & Industries, Joint Commission, State WPV Laws, and the Dept. of Health all recognize that programs like PSTI's are excellent preventive measures to reduce crime, violence and aggression in the workplace.

www.PersonalSafetyTraining.com

PSTI Offers

On-Site Training (we will come to you!) No need to send staff away for training. PSTI will come to your place of business and train your staff.

Train-the-Trainer (Instructor Seminars)
The most cost effective way to implement PSTI training courses to your organization. We can come to you for instructor courses or you can send staff to one of our upcoming seminars.

Combo Classes
Combination classes are where basic training and instructor training are combined during on-site training. It is a great way to introduce PSTI training with our initial instruction and then continue on with your own instructors.

E-Learning
Are you looking for a healthcare solution to integrate a workplace violence prevention program in order to meet compliance standards for both State and Federal guidelines? AVADE® E-learning offers a great solution to give your staff an introductory, yet comprehensive training program that can be completed as needed.

About Us
Personal Safety Training Inc. is committed to providing the finest level of training and service to you and your employees. Whether you are an individual, or represent an agency, we have the Basic and Instructor Course Certifications that YOU need.

Contact Us

Personal Safety Training Inc.
P.O. Box 2957, Coeur d' Alene, ID 83816
(208) 664-5551—Fax (208) 664-5556

Multiple training options for your organization:

- **2 hr. Intro Courses**
- **1/2 Day Training Sessions**
- **One Day Classes**
- **Two Day Classes**
- **Train-the-Trainer (Instructor Classes)**

PSTI serves a variety of industries:

Healthcare	Corporate	Security	Gaming	Churches

TRAINING COURSES FOR YOU AND YOUR AGENCY

SOCS® (Security Oriented Customer Service)

SOCS® training teaches staff how to identify and provide great customer service while maintaining safety in the workplace. The core concept of the training is to be able to provide excellent service without having to think about it. Creating habits, skills, and taking action for exceptional customer service is the goal of the SOCS® training program.
www.SOCStraining.com

DTS™ (Defensive Tactics System)

The DTS™ training program covers basic defensive tactics, control techniques and defensive interventions. Course includes stance, movement, escort techniques, take-downs, defensive blocking, active defense skills, weapon retention, handcuffing, post incident response and documentation and much-much more.

AVADE® Personal Safety Training

Buy the ultimate book on HOW to keep you and your family safe. Call us for training. The training program is designed to increase your overall safety in all environments. The curriculum is based David Fowler's book, *Be Safe Not Sorry—the Art and Science of keeping YOU and your Family safe from crime and violence.*

AVADE® Workplace Violence Prevention

The Workplace Violence Prevention Training is offered as a Basic and Instructor level course for private corporations, healthcare, security companies' and any agency wanting to educate, prevent and mitigate the risk of violence to their employees.

Pepper Spray Defense™ Training

Tactical and Practical concepts of when and how to use pepper spray in a variety of environmental situations. Aerosol Pepper is a great less-than-lethal control and defense option for agencies that encounter violence and aggression.

Defense Baton™ Training Techniques

Training in the use of an expandable baton, straight stick or riot control baton. Techniques and topics in this training include: vulnerable areas of the body, stance, movement, blocks, control holds, counter strikes, draws and retention techniques.

Handcuffing Tactics™

Training in the use of plastic, chain or hinged handcuffs. Standing, kneeling and prone handcuffing techniques are covered. In this training course you will also learn DT fundamentals, proper positioning, nomenclature, risk factors and post incident response and documentation.

HDTS™ (Healthcare Defensive Tactics System)

The HDTS™ training program for healthcare covers basic defensive tactics, control techniques and defensive interventions. Course includes stance, movement, escort techniques, take-downs, team intervention, defensive blocking, active defense skills, weapon retention, patient restraint techniques, post incident response and documentation and much-much more.

SIRS™ (Security Incident Reporting System)

A training program that teaches officers how to effectively and intelligently write security incident reports. Documentation of security incidents is absolutely critical to your agency's ability to track and trend, reduce liability and share vital information. If you're like most agencies–you know that proper, structured, effective and reliable reports save time, money and allow you to track incidents and reduce liability risk.

AVADE® Violence in the Workplace

Buy the book on HOW to be safe in the work-place. This is the text based on the AVADE® training system. Can't come to a class, at least get the book! The knowledge contained in these pages will teach YOU awareness, vigilance, avoidance, defensive interventions and escape strategies for your place of business.

PSTI TRAINING PRODUCTS

Instructor Manuals

Student Manuals

Training Weapons

PSTI MEDIA

Check out our videos

Write a review

Contact us today for training for YOU or your Agency!

Personal Safety Training Inc.
(208) 664-5551 ~
www.PersonalSafetyTraining.com

Check out PSTI on Social Media

LinkedIn

Google

Facebook

YouTube

Twitter

Made in the USA
San Bernardino, CA
23 June 2017